CompTIA® Cloud Essentials™ (Exam CLO-001)

CompTIA® Cloud Essentials™ (Exam CLO-001)

Part Number: 085195
Course Edition: 1.01

NOTICES

HELP US IMPROVE OUR COURSEWARE

Your comments are important to us. Please contact us at Element K Press LLC, 1-800-478-7788, 500 Canal View Boulevard, Rochester, NY 14623, Attention: Product Planning, or through our Web site at **http://support.elementkcourseware.com**.

CompTIA® Cloud Essentials™ (Exam CLO-001)

About This Course

The dynamic business environment today may increase IT demands tremendously. And, you need to meet the demands to ensure the survival of your organization in the market. Needless to say, you must make plans to meet the demands within limited resources of finance, people, and technology. This is exactly what cloud computing can provide to your business. In this course, you will weigh the pros and cons of cloud computing to make effective decisions in meeting the IT challenges.

With IT woven into the effective functioning of every business, there is a greater dependency on the ready availability and deployability of IT infrastructure. Cloud computing offers solutions that enable businesses optimize their IT usage. Therefore, it is critical that every IT and business specialist gains insight into the advantages and disadvantages offered by this business computing model.

Course Description

Target Student

The CompTIA® Cloud Essentials™ Specialty certification is relevant to IT specialists, IT technical services specialists, IT relationship managers, IT architects, consultants, business and IT management, business process owners, and analysts.

Course Prerequisites

This course is the first step on a training path that can lead to a technical career dealing with cloud computing. CompTIA® recommends that a candidate have at least six months of experience in an IT environment, with direct involvement in IT-related tasks, responsibilities and/or decision-making. It is also recommended that the candidate take the following course: *Introduction to Network Design and Management.*

Course Objectives

In this course, you will weigh the pros and cons of cloud computing to make effective decisions and meet IT challenges.

You will:
* Learn the fundamental concepts of cloud computing.
* Learn the business aspects and impact of cloud computing.

- Differentiate the types of cloud solutions and the adoption measures needed for each.
- Identify the technical challenges and the mitigation measures involved in cloud computing.
- Identify the steps to successfully adopt cloud services.
- Identify the basic concepts of ITIL and describe how the ITIL framework is useful in the implementation of cloud computing in an organization.
- Identify the possible risks involved in cloud computing and the risk mitigation measures, and you will also identify the potential cost considerations for the implementation of cloud and its strategic benefits.

How to Use This Book

As a Learning Guide

This book is divided into lessons and topics, covering a subject or a set of related subjects. In most cases, lessons are arranged in order of increasing proficiency.

The results-oriented topics include relevant and supporting information you need to master the content. Each topic has various types of activities designed to enable you to practice the guidelines and procedures as well as to solidify your understanding of the informational material presented in the course.

At the back of the book, you will find a glossary of the definitions of the terms and concepts used throughout the course. You will also find an index to assist in locating information within the instructional components of the book.

In the Classroom

This book is intended to enhance and support the in-class experience. Procedures and guidelines are presented in a concise fashion along with activities and discussions. Information is provided for reference and reflection in such a way as to facilitate understanding and practice.

Each lesson may also include a Lesson Lab or various types of simulated activities. You will find the files for the simulated activities along with the other course files on the enclosed CD-ROM. If your course manual did not come with a CD-ROM, please go to **http:// www.elementk.com/courseware-file-downloads** to download the files. If included, these interactive activities enable you to practice your skills in an immersive business environment, or to use hardware and software resources not available in the classroom. The course files that are available on the CD-ROM or by download may also contain sample files, support files, and additional reference materials for use both during and after the course.

As a Teaching Guide

Effective presentation of the information and skills contained in this book requires adequate preparation. As such, as an instructor, you should familiarize yourself with the content of the entire course, including its organization and approaches. You should review each of the student activities and exercises so you can facilitate them in the classroom.

Throughout the book, you may see Instructor Notes that provide suggestions, answers to problems, and supplemental information for you, the instructor. You may also see references to "Additional Instructor Notes" that contain expanded instructional information; these notes appear in a separate section at the back of the book. PowerPoint slides may be provided on the included course files, which are available on the enclosed CD-ROM or by download from http://www.elementk.com/courseware-file-downloads. The slides are also referred to in the text. If you plan to use the slides, it is recommended to display them during the corresponding content as indicated in the instructor notes in the margin.

The course files may also include assessments for the course, which can be administered diagnostically before the class, or as a review after the course is completed. These exam-type questions can be used to gauge the students' understanding and assimilation of course content.

As a Review Tool

Any method of instruction is only as effective as the time and effort you, the student, are willing to invest in it. In addition, some of the information that you learn in class may not be important to you immediately, but it may become important later. For this reason, we encourage you to spend some time reviewing the content of the course after your time in the classroom.

As a Reference

The organization and layout of this book make it an easy-to-use resource for future reference. Taking advantage of the glossary, index, and table of contents, you can use this book as a first source of definitions, background information, and summaries.

Course Icons

Icon	Description
	A **Caution Note** makes students aware of potential negative consequences of an action, setting, or decision that are not easily known.
	Display Slide provides a prompt to the instructor to display a specific slide. Display Slides are included in the Instructor Guide only.
	An **Instructor Note** is a comment to the instructor regarding delivery, classroom strategy, classroom tools, exceptions, and other special considerations. Instructor Notes are included in the Instructor Guide only.
	Notes Page indicates a page that has been left intentionally blank for students to write on.
	A **Student Note** provides additional information, guidance, or hints about a topic or task.
	A **Version Note** indicates information necessary for a specific version of software.

Course Requirements

Hardware

You will need a computer for the instructor to display course overheads. Computers are not mandatory for students, but will be helpful for them to browse the Internet while discussing specific points. The following system requirements are the minimum suggested for this course:

- Intel® Pentium® IV with 300 MHz (or better).
- At least 512 MB of RAM.
- CD-ROM drive.

- A monitor capable of 1024 x 768 screen resolution and 32-bit color display.
- Display system to project the instructor's computer screen
- Internet connection.

Software

- Microsoft® Windows 7
- Microsoft® Office® PowerPoint®

Class Setup

In preparation for the class, you will need a PC capable of projecting the overheads provided on the CD-ROM. You may use the viewer that is provided on the disk, or copy the files locally and display them using PowerPoint.

1. Install Microsoft® Windows® 7 and Microsoft® Office® PowerPoint® according to the software manufacturer's installation instructions.

2. Insert the CD-ROM that accompanies this course into the CD-ROM drive.

3. On the course CD-ROM, run the **085195dd.exe** self-extracting file. This will install a folder named **085195Data** on your **C:** drive. This folder contains all the data files that you will use to complete this course.

List of Additional Files

Printed with each activity is a list of files students open to complete that activity. Many activities also require additional files that students do not open, but are needed to support the file(s) students are working with. These supporting files are included with the student data files on the course CD-ROM or data disk. Do not delete these files.

1 | Introduction to Cloud Computing

Lesson Time: 1 hour(s)

Lesson Objectives:

In this lesson, you will learn the fundamental concepts of cloud computing.

You will:

- Gain an insight into the basic components of cloud computing.
- Describe the evolution of cloud computing.
- Identify specialized types of cloud services.

Introduction

With cloud computing service delivery models gaining momentum in the business world today, you may be wondering if cloud services may be a solution to your IT challenges. As you know, the IT need of every organization is unique. Cloud computing offers business benefits to organizations that have deployed it. Therefore, you have to understand the pros and cons of the technology. In this lesson, you will learn the fundamental concepts of cloud computing.

Information Technology (IT) today has become integral to the functioning of every business. Whether it is communicating via email or doing business through e-commerce, all organizations rely heavily on their computers, smart devices, and networking systems to conduct everyday business activities. Cloud computing solutions offer businesses several opportunities and benefits to optimize the organizations' IT usage. Therefore, gaining insight into the concepts, functioning and impact of the cloud will go a long way in shaping your business decisions.

TOPIC A
Overview of Cloud Computing

You will need to understand the fundamentals of cloud computing before you consider deploying it. In this topic, you will familiarize yourself with the underlying components that make the cloud, and also identify the main components of the cloud.

Before sprouting wings and taking off towards the cloud, it is important to lay a solid foundation to take off from. To do that, you need to get the basics right, so that deploying a cloud computing interface based on your needs becomes much easier.

Cloud Computing

Definition:

Cloud computing is a business computing model that delivers easy-to-use, on-demand network access to a pool of computing resources, including software, infrastructure, and hardware facilities over a network. This "pay-per-use" model helps an organization to use resources as and when needed, and pay only for the facilities and the time for which resources have been used. These services can be quickly provisioned and managed with minimal effort.

Example:

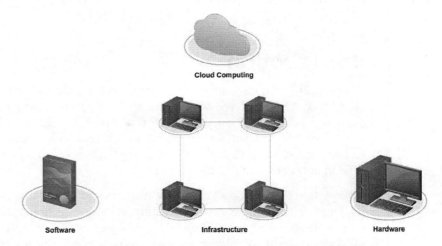

Figure 1-1: Different computing resources associated with the cloud.

Components of the Cloud

Cloud computing is made up of multiple components that combine to make up a cloud service. A client, network, platform, and web APIs are some of the critical components.

Component	Description
Client	The interface that is connected to the cloud through the network.
Web Application	An application that is accessed over a network.

Component	Description
Cloud Services	The services that are obtained on an interface through a single network or a combination of networks.

Clients

Definition:

A *client* is an interface with which a user or another application accesses cloud services. It consists of hardware and/or software that are designed for delivery of cloud services. The client computer has its own processor, memory and storage, and can maintain some of its own resources and perform its own tasks and processing. Any type of computer on a network can function as a client of another computer from time to time. The client hardware can access the cloud interface using operating systems, databases, middleware, and applications through cloud APIs and browsers.

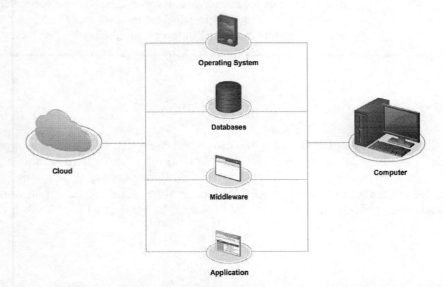

Figure 1-2: A client computer that can access different computing resources through the cloud.

Example:

Client types can include computers, mobiles, smart phones, tablets and servers.

Figure 1-3: Different types of clients.

Types of Clients

There are different types of clients in terms of hardware and application software. However, all types of cloud clients are divided into three broad categories.

Category	Description
Mobile	These clients include devices such as laptops and mobile devices, including PDAs or smartphones like iPhone® or BlackBerry® to connect to the cloud and access applications.
Thin	These are computers that do not have internal hard drives. The server does all the processing and the thin client displays the results. These kinds of client devices do not have any applications stored on end-user systems and can be used when only cloud-based services have to be accessed. Examples of a thin client include X Window System, Citrix, and Microsoft Terminal Services.
Thick	These are workstation computers which use a web browser as an interface to connect to the cloud. In these instances, there will be critical applications that are still installed on the end user's computer. To access applications that are stored in the cloud, thick clients will use browsers.

Networks

Definition:

A *network* is the connecting nexus between the cloud and users. There are several types of networks, such as the Internet, and Virtual Private Network, that vary based on the levels of complexity. The Internet is the most basic choice for cloud connectivity. Employing advanced network services can benefit both the service provider and the client. But computing requirements of organizations differ, and therefore they will need to connect to the cloud in different ways.

Example:

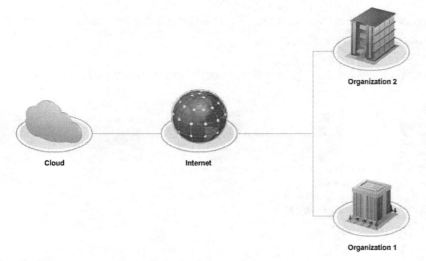

Figure 1-4: Network connection in a cloud infrastructure.

The Web Application Programming Interface

A *Web Application Programming Interface (API)* is a set of programming instructions, protocols, and tools for accessing a web-based program. Software based organizations release their APIs to the public so that other software developers can design products that are powered by their service. APIs are generally designed for programmers because all programs with similar functionalities can use the same API. There are several APIs, and their usage will depend on the cloud provider.

Key Characteristics of Cloud Computing

The cloud computing model encompasses certain characteristics that define its operation and usage. The key characteristics of cloud computing can be classified into five categories: On-demand self-service, Broad network access, Resource pooling, Rapid elasticity, and Measured service.

Characteristic	Description
Elasticity	Automatic scaling of resources, either up or down, is done based on specific requirement.
Access to the network	Resources are accessed over the network through standard client interfaces such as mobile phones, laptops, and PDAs.
On-demand Self-service	Computing capabilities, including the server time and network storage, are accessed as and when required, from a single source. The interaction with the service provider requires minimal human interaction.
Pooling of resources	Computing resources that are pooled to serve multiple users are deployed using a multi-tenant model. According to the need, the physical and virtual resources are dynamically assigned and reassigned. The service is provided independent of the location, and the user may not be necessarily aware of the exact location of the country or state.
Measurement of services	The service model should control and optimize resource usage by providing metered billing.

Types of Cloud

Cloud computing is basically a service that provides an organization with a variety of ways to increase its IT capacity and/or functionality, without the need for additional infrastructure, personnel, and software. There are three different types of cloud such as *IaaS*, *PaaS*, and *SaaS*. The adoption of cloud services is based on an organization's computing and storage requirements.

IaaS   SaaS   PaaS

Figure 1-5: The three main types of cloud.

Type of Cloud	Provides Access To
Infrastructure as a Service (IaaS)	Computer and storage resources maintained on a service provider's environment. Examples of existing IaaS services are AWS, SQL Azure, Rackspace, and IBM.
Platform as a Service (PaaS)	Platforms, such as web applications, database servers, enterprise service buses and other middleware, with associated security mechanisms, that let you develop, test and deploy applications. Examples of existing PaaS services are Force.com, Google App Engine, Windows Azure (Platform).
Software as a Service (SaaS)	Applications, such as customer relationship management software, running on the service provider's environment. The services are released in line with the changing demands. Examples of existing SaaS services are Google Docs, Salesforce CRM, and SAP Business by Design.

Cloud Deployment Models

The IT needs of every organization are diverse and unique. Cloud computing provides service delivery models to suit specific organizational requirements. Utilization of the cloud can be classified into four broad categories.

Deployment Model	Description
Private	Provides hosted services internally to a limited number of people, or an organization that creates and maintains it. In this model, there are fewer restrictions on network bandwidth, security lapses, and other legal intricacies because the resources are maintained on-site. eBay is an example of a private cloud.
Public	Provides resources that are dynamically provisioned on a self-service basis over the Internet, via web services. The public cloud infrastructure is made available to the general public through an off-site third-party service provider.
Hybrid	Stores most of an organization's critical data in-house and moves the rest of the data to the cloud. This type of cloud deployment combines the security of a private cloud service with the efficiency of a public cloud service.
Community	Enables organizations having similar requirements, to share computing resources as opposed to each organization subscribing to a separate cloud service. The cloud may be managed by the organizations or a third-party and may exist on or off-premise.

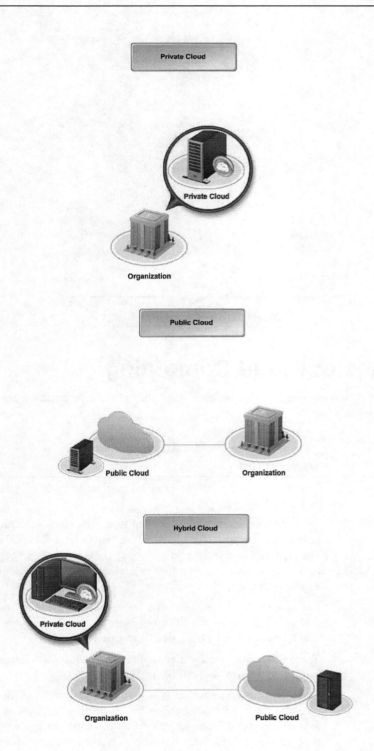

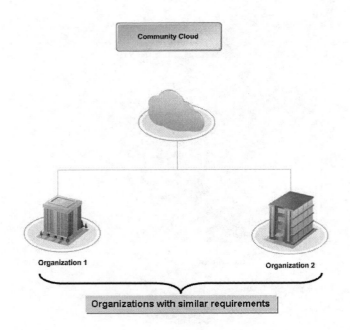

Advantages of Cloud Computing

The advantages of cloud computing can be classified into three categories: economic, agility, and efficiency benefits.

Advantage	Description
Economic	The pay-per-use principle of cloud computing reduces your capital expenses or CAPEX.
	In an on-premise model, you need to incur extensive capital to build data centers and to purchase hardware and software licenses. In contrast, when you deploy cloud computing you pay only for the resources you consume during your operation, turning capital expenses (CAPEX) into operational expenses (OPEX).
	Because the hardware and software resources reside on the cloud, the cloud provider has the responsibility of maintaining the resources. This enables you to reduce your IT resource and manpower.
Agility	The agility provided by cloud computing solutions reduces the time it takes to plan, purchase, and configure IT resources.
	Suppose your organization is launching a new website for customers and you need to test its functioning before hosting it. You can handle the problem in two ways. You can either buy the software license for a load testing tool, or hire a third party who can perform the testing for you. Both these solutions can consume considerable time and money. On the other hand, you can opt for cloud computing, wherein you use an open source load test hosted on the cloud, which significantly reduces the time to configure the system.

Advantage	Description
Efficiency	When the demand for resources increases, the cloud scales up to meet the demand. The scalability makes IT management simpler because a significant portion of your resources reside on the cloud and are managed by the cloud provider. When you own a data center, you need to manage large power and cooling facilities. In addition, you need to develop standard operating procedures to manage the data center. With cloud computing, you can simply rely on the cloud provider to provide such complex tasks, and you can focus more on your core business.

ACTIVITY 1-1
Identifying the Fundamentals of Cloud Computing

Scenario:

In this activity, you will review your knowledge of the various components that comprise the cloud.

1. **Which component is a set of programming instructions and standards for accessing a web-based program?**

   a) Platform

   b) Web API

   c) Web Browser

   d) Web Application

2. **Identify the client that uses a web browser as an interface to connect to the cloud.**

   a) Thick

   b) Thin

   c) Mobile

   d) Web API

TOPIC B
Evolution of the Cloud

You now have an idea of what cloud computing is all about, what it comprises, and what kinds of services the technology can offer. Depending on the requirements of your organization, you can choose to adopt one of the several cloud computing solutions. You may now want to know about the various cloud service delivery models in detail so that you can make a decision about deploying the appropriate cloud service. In this topic, you will identify the various cloud service models.

Just as you need to know what is available in a store before you make a purchase, you will need to know the various cloud services available for deployment. While cloud computing brings in distinct advantages in several business scenarios, it needs to be deployed only after a thorough study of the available cloud services and the service providers.

The History of Cloud Computing

Cloud computing has evolved through a number of phases. As the idea of computation being delivered as a public utility was being generated, the cloud was amended into its different forms. The introduction of "Intergalactic Computer Network" in 1969 with a vision of inter-connecting and accessing programs with everyone, at any location, and at any time, paved the way in deriving the concept of cloud computing. The key factors that enabled the evolution of cloud computing are the matured virtualization technology, development of universal high-speed bandwidth, and software inter-operability standards.

The introduction of Salesforce.com in 1999 was one of the first milestones for cloud comput-ing. It pioneered the concept of delivering enterprise applications through a simple website which paved the way for software firms to deliver applications over the internet. The next development was Amazon Web Services in 2002, which provided cloud-based services such as storage, computation, and human intelligence. Amazon then launched "Elastic Compute cloud (EC2)" in 2006 which is a commercial web service that allows small companies and individu-als to rent computers on which their own applications run.

Another milestone in cloud computing was the arrival of Web 2.0 in 2009 where Google and other service providers started to offer browser-based enterprise applications.

On-Demand Computing Solution Models

On-demand computing solutions form the basis of today's cloud computing service delivery model. On-demand computing is a business model in which computing resources are made available based on user needs. *Grid computing* and *Utility computing* are the initial forms of on-demand computing.

Grid computing facilitates sharing of a complex computational task across multiple computers. Computers from the same or various geographical locations are networked together to form a grid. In this model, the resources of several computers are utilized to complete a single task at any given point in time.

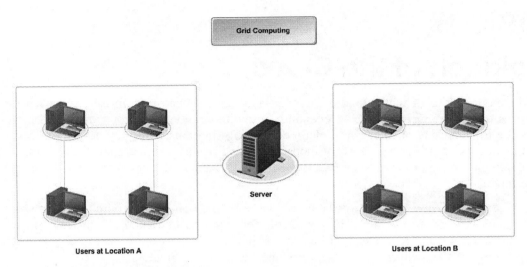

Figure 1-6: *The Grid Computing Model.*

The second computing model is utility computing. In this model, the service provider provides computing and infrastructure resources to a customer and charges only for the usage. The third computing model, *Software as a Service (SaaS)*, deploys software over a network, typically the Internet. Cloud computing is the next generation computing model that combines the computing and business concepts of grid, utility, and SaaS computing.

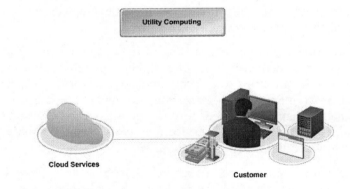

Figure 1-7: *The Utility Computing Model.*

Cloud Computing vs. Virtualization

Virtualization is the process of creating virtual replicas or virtual machines (VMs) of computing resources, such as a physical computer. For example, you can create several virtual servers from a single physical server. The most interesting part of virtualization is that virtual servers share the underlying hardware resources of physical servers, obviating the need to maintain an extensive hardware system.

Cloud computing takes virtualization to the next level by providing rapid provisioning and de-provisioning of computing resources, combined with the pay-per-use benefit. An application deployed on the cloud paves the way for utilization of new resources by scaling up when the demand is increasing. Once the demand drops, the additional resources are taken offline.

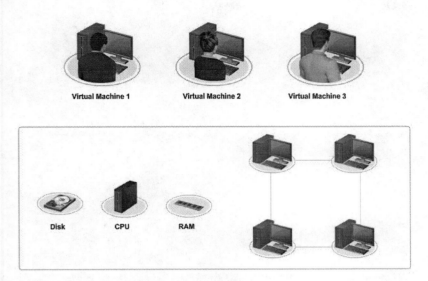

Figure 1-8: *Virtual machines sharing the underlying hardware resources.*

Virtualization and Hardware Independence

Cloud computing facilitates the efficient usage of resources and applications through virtualization. Virtualization supports running of multiple virtual machines on a single physical machine, with each machine sharing the resources of one physical computer across multiple environments. This means that services can still function independent of hardware, while being secure and scalable. This resource optimization drives greater flexibility in the organization, thus resulting in lower capital and operational costs.

Cloud Computing vs. Grid and Utility Computing

Grid computing is a model that allows you to use the computing resources available within the specified grid at any point in time, and harness idle computer power. Within a grid, one large job is divided into many small portions and executed on multiple machines. As the small individual tasks are completed, the results are collated by the controlling unit to form a cohesive output.

In the grid computing model, the user bears the expenses for maintaining the computing resources in the grid even when the resources are not used. Cloud computing also harnesses idle computing power; whereby the user can utilize multiple resources over the network to accomplish a task and pay only for the usage, without the need to invest in capital upfront. While grid computing also offers computing power, cloud computing isn't restricted to just computing power.

Utility computing often requires a cloud-like infrastructure because it focuses on the business model on which the computing services are provided. Utility computing works on the principle that the utilization of a central pool of computing resources can be metered and billed on the basis of CPU Cycles, Storage GBs, and Network data transfer GBs. Cloud computing extends the metering and "pay-per-use" model beyond computing and storage to software applications.

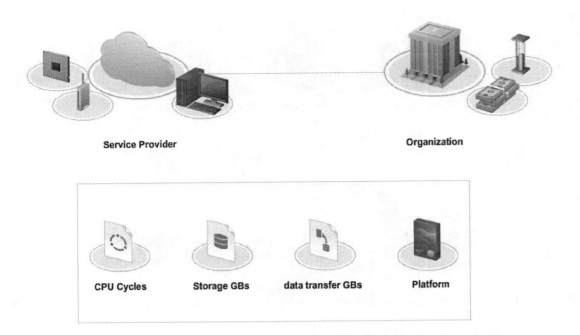

Figure 1-9: *Different computing resources that can be billed and metered.*

Cloud Computing vs. the Client-Server Model

A *client-server model* is a network in which servers provide resources to clients. Typically, there is at least one server providing central authentication services. Servers also provide access to shared files, printers, hardware storage, and applications. In client-server networks, processing power, management services, and administrative functions can be concentrated when needed, while clients can still perform many basic end-user tasks on their own. In the client-server model, additional investment is required for accelerated deployment of new resources to meet sudden changes during demands.

When a user runs an application from the cloud, it is part of a client-server application. However, cloud computing can provide increased performance, flexibility, and significant cost savings because the application hosting and support is the responsibility of the cloud service provider.

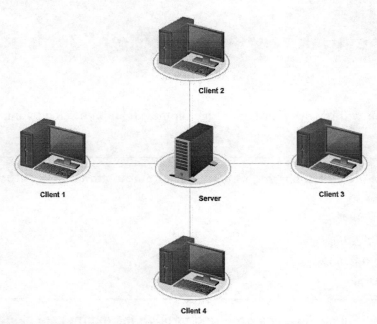

Figure 1-10: *The client-server model.*

Cloud Computing vs. the Peer-to-Peer Model

A *peer-to-peer model* is a network in which resource sharing, processing, and communications control are completely decentralized. All clients on the network are equal in terms of providing and using resources, and users are authenticated by each individual workstation. Peer-to-peer networks are easy and inexpensive to implement. Unlike cloud computing, they are only practical in very small organizations, due to the lack of central data storage and administration. The downsides of the peer-to-peer model can be overcome by adopting a hybrid approach of cloud computing, with servers that are dedicated for management, storage, and monitoring.

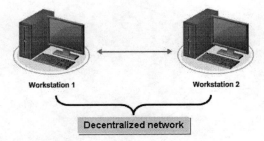

Figure 1-11: *The Peer-to-Peer Model.*

ACTIVITY 1-2
Understanding the Evolution of Cloud Computing

Scenario:
In this activity, you will review your knowledge on the evolution of cloud computing.

1. **Which model facilitates sharing of a complex computational task across multiple computers?**
   a) Client-Server
   b) Peer-to-Peer
   c) Grid Computing
   d) Virtualization

2. **True or False? All applications accessed through the Internet are cloud applications.**
   ___ True
   ___ False

TOPIC C
Specialized Cloud Services

You now have a basic knowledge about the components and models of cloud computing. You may now want to know about the other types of cloud services so that you can make a decision about deploying the appropriate cloud computing model. In this topic, you will identify specialized cloud services.

Imagine having to work with a gadget without knowing its features. You will not be able to leverage and exploit the gadget's strengths unless you explore and identify its unique features. Similarly, you need to be aware of different cloud services, so that you can decide on the type to adopt and how each type can be beneficial to an organization.

Distributed Computing as a Service

Distributed computing is a method of performing a consolidated function with the help of multiple resources that are available in different locations. It is a web service that enables businesses to easily and cost-effectively process vast amounts of data. Distributed computing as a service is a hosted framework that runs on the web-scale infrastructure thereby helping to perform data-intensive tasks of applications. It improves the performance of the system, checks for the availability of the resources, reduces the cost of computation, and allows interaction between resources.

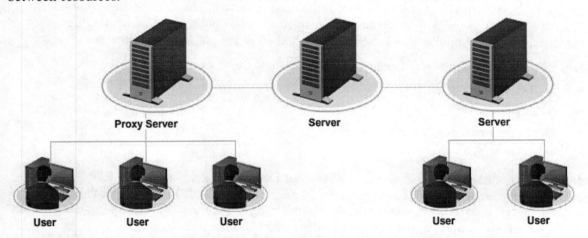

Figure 1-12: A distributed environment where various functions of multiple users are aggregated.

Distributed File System and Database

A *distributed file system (DFS)* is a system of organizing files and directories across multiple computers in a network. The files can be accessed by number of users across the network. DFS helps to easily distribute files to many computers, and also provides a centralized storage system.

A *distributed database* is one in which portions of a database are stored in multiple computers located in the same physical location, or over a network. Users can access the distributed database with the help of a DBMS that manages the operations on databases. An example of distributed database is HBase, which is a Hadoop based distributed database.

Hadoop

The Apache Hadoop software library is a framework that uses a programming model to process huge amounts of data across multiple computers. It is designed to scale up from single servers to hundreds of machines where each machine offers local computation, processing, and storage. Hadoop also detects and handles failure, which results in delivery of high level of service to multiple computers.

MapReduce

The Apache Hadoop library, along with the MapReduce framework, allows for the distributed computation of applications that parallely processes huge data on the cloud. A MapReduce job usually splits the input data-set into independent chunks which are processed by the map tasks in a completely parallel manner. The framework sorts the outputs of the maps, which are then input to reduced tasks. Typically both the input and the output of the job are stored in a file system. The framework takes care of scheduling tasks, monitoring them and re-executing the failed tasks.

Databases as a Service

Databases form a foundation for most of the enterprise applications. In most organizations, database services for applications are provided by installing the required hardware and software, on-premise. Modern databases have advanced features and functionality where they can be used to provide a larger, shared service to the enterprise as a whole. This scheme allows multiple applications to simultaneously access a single database running on a cluster of machines. The applications are isolated from each other, and explicit database processing by the applications is performed as a centralized database service, also termed *Database-as-a-Service (DBaaS)*. By adopting DBaaS, an organization can optimize the computing density, manageability, and complexity of the hardware and software platform combination.

DBaaS provides a number of benefits to organizations. Some of them are:

- Higher availability of resources
- Savings in cost
- Better service through centralized management
- Reduced risk

One example of DBaaS is the Amazon Relational Database Service (Amazon RDS) that enables instances of MySQL to be provisioned and scaled with all low-level administrative requirements. Amazon RDS automatically patches database software, backs up the database for a user-defined retention period, and also enables point-in-time recovery.

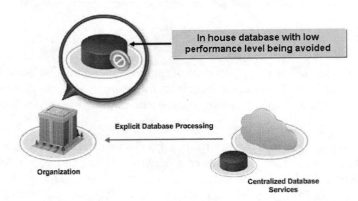

In house database with low performance level being avoided

Explicit Database Processing

Organization

Centralized Database Services

Figure 1-13: An organization adopting DBaaS for explicit database processing.

Open Source Distributed Databases

Distributed databases provide a means to store data remotely, in addition to providing services such as publishing and archival through centralization. It supports very high data availability levels at all times. Distributed databases are also available as open source.

Some of the examples of open source distributed databases are CouchDB, MongoDB, Cassandra, Hypertable, HBase, Voldemort and Hadoop. CouchDB is used when lots of snapshotting is required. MongoDB is desirable when there are high performance requirements and high update rates. Cassandra is capable of high scaling without departing from the mainstream database technology.

Cache as a Service

Caching is the buffering of vital data to speed up the process of information retrieval, instead of fetching the data from the original server. Dynamic data service is an important part of cloud services and as such, *Cache as a Service* is instrumental. Cache as a Service adds an important advantage to an organization by serving data faster and more efficiently. Cache as a Service is provided by means of memcached. Memcached is a memory object caching system that alleviates database load, thereby speeding up dynamic web applications.

Parallelism as a Service

Parallelism refers to the ability to simultaneously perform more than one action or process more than one event. A cloud is made up of numerous virtual resources that can perform multiple actions or run multiple applications in parallel. Cloud computing can provide parallel computing, or *parallelism as a service*, by leveraging its multiple resources to execute and process multiple tasks at the same time, without any fluctuation or disruption in the speed or quality of the service.

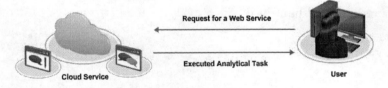

Figure 1-14: The two layers through which parallelism is executed.

Sharding

Definition:

Sharding is a process of breaking a large database into a number of smaller databases across servers. A sharded environment improves the performance and output of high-transaction, and large database-centric business applications. In a cloud environment, sharding helps in improving the search performance by reducing the index size of the database. DBaaS service providers offer sharded environments in the cloud by horizontally scaling up resources.

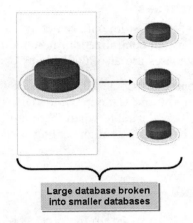

Figure 1-15: A sharded database.

Example:

Some of the sharding schemes that are used in a cloud environment are dbShards, Hibernate ORM, and MongoDB.

The Database Profiler

Definition:

A database profiler analyzes source databases for inconsistencies in structure, content, relationships, and derivation rules of data to avoid an unpredictable implementation effort. It profiles these databases, examines the data quality in them, and then highlights any predictable issues that may arise.

Example:

MongoDB has a profiling tool built in it which analyzes the performance of database operations.

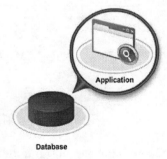

Figure 1-16: A profiler that analyzes the database.

ACTIVITY 1-3
Identifying the Specialized Cloud Services

Scenario:

In this activity, you will review your knowledge of the specialized services of cloud computing.

1. **What are the benefits of DBaaS? (Choose all that apply.)**

   a) Higher availability of resources

   b) Better service

   c) Reduced risks

   d) High costs

2. **True or False? Distributed computing helps to perform data-intensive tasks for applications.**

   ___ True

   ___ False

Lesson 1 Follow-up

In this lesson, you described the various aspects of cloud computing. This knowledge will enable you to relate the use of the cloud technology with your business and IT needs. You also described the infrastructure and interface components of cloud computing. This will help you to deploy cloud services and effectively connect to the cloud.

1. **What kinds of cloud services will you use in your organization and why?**

2. **What characteristics of cloud computing might attract your organization? Why?**

2 | Business Value of Cloud Computing

Lesson Time: 1 hour(s), 45 minutes

Lesson Objectives:

In this lesson, you will learn the business aspects and impact of cloud computing.

You will:

- Ascertain the business need for cloud computing.
- Identify the scalability characteristics of cloud computing.
- Identify the concerns and features of cloud security.
- Discuss the impact of cloud computing on business.

Introduction

You are familiar with the different types of cloud services. The impact of implementing cloud services will enable easier manageability, and less maintenance of IT resources to meet the fluctuating demands of business organizations. In this lesson, you will analyze the business aspects and impact of cloud computing.

In today's corporate scenario, IT has evolved to become an indispensable part of the everyday operation of an organization. However, the challenges associated with selecting, installing, maintaining, and managing IT solutions vary for different types of companies. To determine if moving to cloud computing is a worthwhile venture for your organization, it is important to discern how the business of different types of companies can benefit from a cloud solution.

TOPIC A
Business Need for Cloud Computing

Being aware of the differences between cloud computing and other business models, you may now want to ascertain how cloud computing caters to the business needs of organizations. In this topic, you will identify some of the constraints that a startup organization, a mid-size organization, and an enterprise face, and how they each can benefit from cloud computing.

Every organization has IT needs, and the constraints in meeting the needs vary from organization to organization. As an IT professional, you need to understand the numerous constraints of a startup, a mid-size, and an established enterprise, and determine what cloud solution best fits your needs.

Business Drivers for Migrating to Cloud Computing

Today's business environment requires that an organization improve its efficiency and reduce costs as well. Cloud computing provides many advantages and benefits by separating computing power needs from the IT barriers of cost, time, quality, scale, and location. The major factors that drive an organization to migrate to cloud services again depend on its specific business priorities. But the important question to answer when evaluating a cloud solution is "what business problems need to be solved?"

Business Driver	Description
Maximizing Cost Efficiencies	From a cost saving perspective, cloud computing can preserve capital, turning a large, upfront capital expenditure into an operational expenditure. Cost savings is realized in an organization because of the cloud's "pay as you go" model.
Planning and Strategy	Cloud computing is not one-size-fits-all. As you review your business needs and priorities, you may find that some applications are a better fit for use in the cloud. The low barrier to entry in terms of capital outlay can make it possible for you to reach new customers across the globe. Further, new customers can come online faster because resources are readily available and scalable.
Improved Time to Market	The scalability of cloud computing allows for shorter development cycles, so the development team can reduce the time to market. The resources you need can be made available with just a request for more resources. This in turn means that the temporary resources needed for certain projects or new product development can move forward without capital investment.
Accommodating Unpredictable Demand	Retail business and financial business in particular are subject to boom times and quiet times in their business cycles. Cloud computing lets you expand and contract IT resources in sync with those cycles. Your requirements determine what you need in a cloud computing solution, along with considerations such as data sensitivity, security levels, and compliance requirements.

SME Business and Cloud Computing

A Small to Medium Enterprise (SME) is a business organization that can be privately owned and would typically have 100 to 1000 employees. To understand the impact cloud computing can have on an organization of this size, consider a fictional example.

Overview:

- Ristell Tech is a mid-sized IT firm that is on an upward curve. Some time back, a server disruption resulted in the loss of some of their important data. Fortunately the damage was stemmed and the loss was not very significant. But this called for a backup plan as a proactive measure to avoid instances of data loss.

Ristell Tech Challenges:

- The cost of additional equipment to store data.
- The higher maintenance cost incurred with an internal data center.
- The cost and security of an off-premise data backup system.

Ristell Tech Solution: Cloud storage to back up data and schedule regular updates over the Internet

Ristell Tech Benefits:

- Reduced maintenance costs.
- Regular data backup which can be retrieved in the event of data loss or failure.
- Reduced storage needs of internal data center.

Large Business and Cloud Computing

A large business, often a commercial corporation, is one which has established itself and is a key player in its space. Because time to market is a major factor for such large companies, missed deadlines mean loss of revenue, drop in market share, and lower stock value. To understand the impact cloud computing can have on an organization of this size, consider a fictional example.

Overview:

- Ristell Pharma is a global pharmaceutical company which has a department dedicated to the research and development of drugs. They recently signed a contract to develop a new drug. The restriction, however, is that they must deliver the drug to the market within 730 days; realistically, it could take closer to 1450 days. This project also requires enormous amounts of computing resources for analysis of research reports and statistics, molecular structure modeling, and tabulating test statistics, all of which has to begin within a month.

Ristell Pharma Challenges:

- Traditional IT infrastructure deployment was inhibiting business.
- Delayed time-to-deliver due to traditional procurement timelines.
- Desire to move from fixed to variable cost model.

Ristell Pharma Solution: Multiple cloud providers. They obtained infrastructure resources from one cloud provider and the platform to build the application from another cloud provider.

Ristell Pharma Benefits:

- Reduced provisioning cycle time
  - New server: 60 days to 3 minutes.

- New collaboration environment: 70 days to 10 minutes.
- 64-node Linux™ cluster: 100 days to 30 minutes.

Start-up Business and Cloud Computing

A startup organization is a business organization that has just entered the market and is looking to establish itself. Usually privately owned, it would have a few employees. A startup can face several hurdles up front, primary among them being setting up the required infrastructure, and financial restraints. To understand the impact cloud computing can have on an organization of this size, consider a fictional example.

Overview:

- Ristell Flights (a fictional organization), is a startup company that offers services to business travellers, whose business model is to predict flight timings of a major carrier by studying and analyzing real time scenarios with historical flight departure and arrival information. To do this, the team has to process large volumes of data, requiring a significant investment to set up servers, data storage systems, and other facilities. Also, the organization has to be in continuous touch with the customers and needs to respond to customers' queries quickly.

Ristell Flights Challenges:

- Capital investment to set up servers, data storage systems, and other IT facilities.
- Procuring, deploying, and managing infrastructure and software resources within a short span of time.

Ristell Flights Solution:

- Cloud-based storage and computing resources for storing and processing huge volumes of data.
- Online discussion forums over cloud platform in two days to respond to customer queries.

Ristell Flights Benefits:

- Reduced capital expenditure.
- Reduced fixed IT infrastructure needs.
- Agility—respond rapidly to business needs.

Types of Business That Benefit from Cloud Computing

The need to provide improved IT services is a driving force for organizations to manage the complex infrastructure and control the cost of acquiring additional resources. The advent of cloud computing proved to be advantageous for automating the provisioning and scheduling of hardware resources to cater to the demands of customers. The size and the business model of an organization determine the benefit level of adopting cloud services.

- **IaaS:** The usually capital constrained small and medium software development companies can realize significant benefit by adopting IaaS because the storage and computing capabilities are offered as a service.

- **PaaS:** The small and medium software development companies, large organizations that carry out small projects, and software start-up organizations can benefit by adopting PaaS. This is because of the simplicity that PaaS facilitates in the process of an application development and deployment. The organizations that adopt PaaS need not spend capital to buy and manage the hardware and software layers.

- **SaaS:** Since SaaS eliminates the process of software maintenance, ongoing operation and support in an organization, any organization which requires standard business process infrastructure, such as CRM, or communication systems will realize a benefit.

Figure 2-1: *The types of organizations that may benefit from different types of cloud services.*

Types of Business That May Not Benefit from Cloud Computing

Though cloud computing benefits an organization with the reduction of cost and effort through outsourcing and automation of essential resource management, there are a few organizations that may not actually benefit from cloud services.

- **IaaS:** Small and Medium non-software organizations may not benefit from adopting IaaS. This is because of the non-availability of technical staff within the organization to handle low level server details. By appointing an expert in the organization for this purpose may result in spending more than required on resources. For example, a micro-brewery would invest heavily in the equipment and resources needed for brewing beers, and may have no need for an IT infrastructure to brew, bottle, and deliver their product.

- **PaaS:** Organizations that work on projects which are extremely sensitive regarding the legality, security, or performance of their assets, may not benefit by adopting PaaS.

- **SaaS:** Large organizations that have already made huge investments on IT may not benefit by adopting SaaS. This would lead to costly and unnecessary redundancy of the existing investments.

Figure 2-2: *The types of organizations that may not benefit from different types of cloud services.*

ACTIVITY 2-1
Understanding the Business Need for Cloud Computing

Scenario:

In this activity, you will review your knowledge on the business needs of cloud computing.

1. **What are the business drivers of cloud computing? (Choose all that apply.)**

   a) Increased time to market

   b) Cost efficiencies maximization

   c) Strategic planning

   d) Accommodation of unpredictable demand

2. **True or False? SaaS provides services to an organization that requires the standard business process infrastructure such as CRM.**

   ___ True

   ___ False

TOPIC B
Cloud Scalability

You are aware of the business needs of cloud computing. Scalability is also a business need, and one of the major factors that drives an organization to move to a cloud environment. In this topic, you will discuss cloud scalability and its types.

Imagine having to work with a gadget without understanding what its features can do. You will not be able to leverage and exploit the gadget's strengths unless you explore and identify its unique attributes. Similarly, you need to be aware of what characteristics the cloud can comprise.

Scalability

Scalability is a vital attribute of cloud computing. It is the capability of the cloud service and application to expand or contract the required computing, networking, and storage resources based on need, without human intervention or additional cost. In software organizations, cloud computing permits an organization's IT division to expand, organize, and run applications to improve its competence, and work quickly without the risk of network server failure. This factor influences an organization's decision to opt for cloud computing, helping it avoid too much money and time being wasted. The term scalability is also referred to as "flexibility" or "elasticity."

Benefits of Scalability

The scalability feature of cloud services provides an organization with inherent efficiency in terms of presentation and resource management. The move from physical computing to virtual computing economically benefits an organization by casting aside physical hardware. It also benefits the development side by providing flexible infrastructure architecture. Since the number of servers that have to be provisioned is not bound by the physical size of the server closet, a whole new way of scaling the infrastructure can be unlocked.

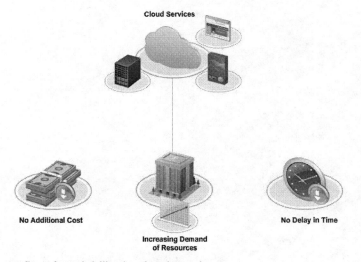

Figure 2-3: The benefits of scalability in cloud services.

Types of Scalability

The types of cloud computing scalability offer efficiency in building an infrastructure that can be easily scaled in the cloud.

Scaling Type	Description
Vertical scaling	Vertical scaling refers to the inclusion of additional resources to an existing node of a system. This might involve additional processors, RAM, or disk space to a server for benefitting the application infrastructure. Vertical scaling also includes adding components for redundancy. Few examples of such components are power supply, fans, and disk drives. This addition of components for redundancy ensures that the machines continue to operate, even if a specific component fails. Adding more servers to a single hardware server is another way of vertical scaling.
	Vertical scaling is also referred to as scaling up.
Horizontal scaling	Horizontal scaling refers to the inclusion of more nodes to a system. This includes adding up another server to the *cluster* of an application server. The additional servers added to the cluster handle the processing of a distributed work in a seamless manner, when the actual server becomes unavailable at a given point of time. Horizontal scaling is also referred to as scaling out.
Diagonal scaling	Diagonal scaling allows both vertical and horizontal scalability. It enables you to add servers dynamically until the limit of diminishing returns is reached. When no more servers can be added, the same server is cloned over and over again to handle more concurrent requests.

Handling Peak Business Load

Cloud computing enables an organization to enhance application performance, ensure availability, and control the associated costs. This means that cloud services provide a scalable framework that balances the collection and supply of variables that are required for making application routing decisions.

By implementing load balancers, cloud services efficiently handle the peak business load that is often encountered. The Load Balancer continuously monitors numerous site-level attributes to ensure optimum management of global traffic. It provides critical business continuity and global disaster recovery support when site-level disruptions and outages occur.

The business benefits of using load balancers in an organization point include reduced cost of application delivery, compliance with government and industry regulations, and meeting customer requirements. Load balancers are generally applied when:

● Access to application variables or instances is greater.

● Connections are required through intelligent services.

● Storage resources are high.

● Services such as DNS, FTP, HTTP, and HTTPS are required.

Scalability with Different Types of Cloud Computing

Cloud services allow organizations to serve larger consumers, solve more complex and challenging problems, access incremental computing resources on-demand, and reduce the risk around complex new projects by starting small, and growing as the need increases. This elastic property differs for different types of cloud services.

Type of Cloud Service	Scalability Level
IaaS	Server and storage resources can be quickly scaled while still ensuring seamless data quality and data profiling.
PaaS	Scaling at the level of back-end databases, workflow management, application servicing, the delivery platform, the source code control application, the version control application, and the dynamic multiple user testing environments can be achieved in PaaS.
SaaS	Scaling at the level of Identity management servers, Application servers, Integration servers, Communication servers, and business services can be done. Administrative services like billing, operations, and support can also be scaled in SaaS.

Spawning Machines

Cloud computing enables large-scale prototyping and load testing. When there is an explicit request for provisioning with additional resources, cloud computing can create new instances of machines in the network by spawning thousands of machines in a fraction of time.

ACTIVITY 2-2

Understanding the Scalability Characteristic of Cloud Computing

Scenario:

In this activity, you will review your knowledge of the scalability characteristic of cloud computing.

---

1. **Which type of scaling involves the addition of additional processors, RAM, or disk space to a server?**

    a) Load Balancing

    b) Vertical Scaling

    c) Horizontal Scaling

    d) Diagonal Scaling

---

2. **True or False? Scalability provides a flexible infrastructure architecture to software organizations.**

    ___ True

    ___ False

TOPIC C
Cloud Security

You have identified the business need of scalability in cloud computing. Security is also a business need, and one of the primary concerns when moving to a cloud environment. In this topic, you will discuss cloud security concerns and security features.

Since every technology has its distinctiveness and peculiarity, it is critical that you understand the security concerns related to cloud computing. This understanding of the security attribute will help in identifying the risk and remedy that cloud computing has to offer.

Security

Cloud computing security involves a framework of policies, technologies, and control units that are deployed to protect data, applications, and the infrastructure of cloud computing. There are a number of security issues that are associated with cloud computing. These issues can relate to security threats cloud providers or customers face.

The security issue with respect to cloud providers relates to the restriction of unauthorized access. Organizations are concerned with the audit policies cloud service providers follow, the physical location of data, and the nationality of users accessing the information. The security control in the cloud is generally implemented by:

● Identifying the assets that are prone to security risks.

● Identifying the threats that could be mounted.

● And identifying measures to counter those issues.

Security Concerns

When customers analyze the advantages and disadvantages of cloud computing and its technology, they are often concerned with the endorsements of risk-control processes and technical mechanisms. Also, customers are inquisitive to learn the level of testing carried out to verify whether the control and service processes function as contemplated. Additionally, they also examine if the vendor can forecast new vulnerabilities, and find a suitable solution. Some of the common concerns that can arise in regard to security are:

● **Location of data:** The organization that has adopted cloud computing may not know where exactly the data is hosted. In fact, they might not even know in which country the data will reside. Expert advice becomes essential with respect to the adherence of local privacy requirements and specific jurisdictions.

● **Segregation of data:** In cloud, the data is stored in a shared environment along with the data of other users. The customer may face the dilemma in designing and testing an effective encryption schema for their data.

● **Data recovery:** If data and the application infrastructure cannot be replicated across multiple sites by the cloud service provider, then it is vulnerable to complete failure. This may raise concerns on cloud provider's ability in restoration of data.

● **Restricted user access:** The processing of outsourced services bypass the physical, logical, and personnel controls, thereby posing an inherent threat to the security of the sensitive data. Therefore, privileged user access is important.

- **Compliance to regulations and audit policies:** The security and integrity of data is an ultimate responsibility of customers, though it is held by a service provider. Audits from an external party and certifications on security are recommended for traditional service providers.

- **Viability for longer time:** The availability of data even after an incident of break-in at the cloud provider's location is still a major concern.

Malware

Cloud computing is being hailed as a flexible, affordable way of offering computer resources to consumers, where the computational power and storage of multiple computers are pooled, and can be shared by multiple users. However, concerns exist about hackers finding ways to insert malicious software into cloud computing systems. Some of the factors that make a cloud infrastructure vulnerable to malware are:

- Homogeneity of computers in a network.

- Unconfirmed code copied from external storage devices.

- Privileged users who can modify internal structures.

Security Features in Cloud Computing

Security features are based on different cloud services.

Service Type	Security Feature
IaaS	With IaaS, it is essential that providers of federated cloud services include, in the SLA, the details about the network topology, the creation of virtual machines, and the pattern in which they are spun down to avoid wastage of resources and uncontrolled access.
PaaS	In PaaS, a vital point to consider is data protection, as data loss is more prevalent in this model due to network outage issues. Service providers should ensure data security by adopting load balancing techniques and encryption standards.
SaaS	The SaaS model focuses on managing access to applications. Service providers should establish a control mechanism to authenticate privileged users before accessing applications. For example, creating passwords for each employee to access cloud services is not possible when all employees in an organization have to access the applications at once. Users who have multiple passwords are at risk of a security threat, and also the cost incurred to create a password for each of them is high. Instead, service providers can create a single sign-on mechanism for users to access both on-line premises and the applications in the cloud.

Customizing Security in the Cloud

As of now, research is limited on the provision of security services in cloud computing because security scales as customer requirements change. Given the unique nature of security offerings, it becomes crucial to customize the security settings depending on the type of cloud service. This can be achieved by opening up the technology infrastructure of cloud services such that:

- Data and computation can be moved to logical zones rather than physical zones.
- Standard-based identity services are provided instead of domain access control.
- Hybrid clouds are supported by security management, and service-oriented architecture.
- Encryption performance and key management are enhanced.

ACTIVITY 2-3

Understanding the Cloud Security Features

Scenario:

In this activity, you will discuss security concerns and security features of cloud computing.

1. **What are the major security concerns with regard to cloud computing? (Choose all that apply.)**

   a) Data integration

   b) Data location

   c) Recovery

   d) Long-term viability

2. **True or False? Cloud security is deployed to protect data, applications, and the infrastructure of cloud computing.**

   ___ True

   ___ False

TOPIC D
Impact of Cloud Computing on Business

It is essential that IT organizations not only evaluate the need for and impact of adopting cloud services, but also leverage the cloud for future growth and a competitive edge. In this topic, you will discuss the impact of cloud computing on business.

The challenges associated with selecting, installing, maintaining, and managing IT solutions vary for different types of companies. To determine if moving to cloud computing is a worthwhile venture for your organization, it is helpful to analyze the business impact of cloud solutions.

Level of Value Provided by Cloud Computing

Cloud computing plays a profitable role in an organization by deploying processing power, storage, computing platforms, and applications over a network, reducing the computational time and costs. From a business perspective, cloud computing provides value to an organization at three different levels. Each level builds on the previous level and requires changes in the existing business processes of an organization. But each level also enables value creation, which is larger than the prior level.

- **Utility Level:** Enterprises can benefit from lower costs and higher service levels through the availability of elastic computing resources and pay-per-use models.

- **Process Transformation Level:** Enterprises can introduce new and improved business processes by leveraging common and scalable assets and the collaborative potential of cloud computing.

- **Business-Model-Innovation Level:** New business models can be created by linking, sharing, and combining resources using cloud computing in an entire business ecosystem.

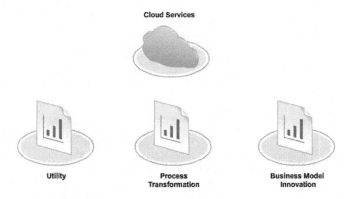

Figure 2-4: The three levels of value provided by cloud.

Utility Level - Basic Level

Definition:

The *Utility level* is the basic level at which an organization can benefit from the availability of elastic computing resources and pay-per-use models of cloud computing. The installation and operating costs are reduced, and higher service levels are guaranteed in terms of efficiency, scale, and focus. The deployment of labor, hardware, software, and power at the Utility level quickly produces bottom-line results.

Item	*Description*
Labor	Most organizations feel that their IT departments spend too much time on keeping the business running. But, these responsibilities are significantly reduced in a cloud environment. Rather than fixing the flaws, IT staff can improve the functionality and features of IT systems, while the heads of an organization work on transforming the business.
Hardware	Companies can benefit from the presumed higher efficiency of cloud service providers. A typical corporate data center needs to be carefully balanced during many competing demands such as optimized utilization, even while managing large spikes in volume, and also delivering high levels of service. Cloud service providers strive to achieve a better balance across these demands by leveraging scale and standardization along with smarter technologies, such as server virtualization. Moreover, they potentially operate at a lower cost than a typical enterprise-IT data center.
Software	An organization's consumption of software is driven by demand. With cloud computing, companies can more easily deploy new applications and adjust usage up or down as compared with a conventional setup. Traditional maintenance and support are performed by the cloud service provider, significantly reducing the operating costs of enterprises.
Power	Enterprises can take advantage of the advanced power-management capabilities of cloud service providers. They can also make use of their renewable energy supplies and other green initiatives that reduce the carbon footprint of computers and servers.

Example:

Our Global Company, a fictional biotechnology company, is an example of a company that has turned to a cloud service platform for its e-mail and calendar programs and a host of other applications for its thousands of employees. At the time of its migration to the cloud-computing model a year ago, the company had around 40 terabytes of e-mail and 3 million scheduled meetings stored in its systems. It was spending tens of millions of dollars on a new data center. Our Global Company avoided that capital expense and reduced its anticipated cost of ownership by several million dollars over the next five years by using cloud service providers and virtualization technologies.

Process Transformation Level - Intermediate Level

Definition:

The *Process Transformation level* is an intermediate level that allows the finance department to conduct transactions more efficiently, researchers to set up and modify their computer models more swiftly, and sales professionals to serve their customers more effectively. Enterprises frequently have a difficult time improving business processes and systems, and the business processes are more often inadequately supported by the underlying technologies, such as an array of different systems and incompatible data structures. The cloud computing model of standardized applications, data formats, and development tools enables the implementation of processes that depend on access to shared data, collaboration, and mobile or remote access.

Finance department   Reseacher   Sales professional

Figure 2-5: *Beneficiaries of the process transformation level.*

Example:

Organizations that are into retail business may benefit most from the process improvements enabled by the cloud computing model. These companies require huge computing resources to analyze the ever growing and expanding data about customers and products. Cloud computing provides the resources to perform real-time analysis of customer behavior, such as spending patterns, and economic incentives such as effects of product placement on sales of merchandise.

Business Model Innovation - Advanced Level

Definition:

The *Business Model Innovation level* is an advanced level that strives to break value chains between organizations to create new and innovative business models. This is achieved by rewiring the way companies operate, making choices of competitive advantage, deriving value out of it, and then co-operating with each other.

Example:

The Pharmaceuticals industry is an example beneficiary of business model innovation enabled by cloud computing. A chain of value is created between the pharmaceutical companies, insurers, physicians, hospitals, and patients because a complete health record of patients is readily available with cloud providers. This results in the fundamental reshaping of processes by the pharmaceutical companies to collaborate on basic, non-proprietary, and expensive research. This actually saves considerable cost on drug discovery, which requires millions of dollars in investment when using traditional methods.

Variable Costs

The impact of cloud computing extends beyond IT operations to the underlying cost structure of IT support of an organization. Cloud computing facilitates a pay-per-use model that allows organizations to transform from a fixed IT costs model to a more variable cost model. The variable cost model of cloud computing has an inherent benefit—aligning IT cost to overall IT usage, where capacity contracts and expands as the business needs of the organization change. The extent that IT operations move to a variable cost structure depends on the organization's architecture and IT demands. Companies with high variability in IT demand greatly benefit from the concept of variable cost of cloud computing.

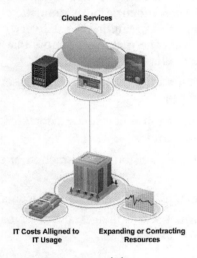

Figure 2-6: *The advantage of a pay-per-use model.*

The variable cost model reduces the business risks of an organization by avoiding the need to make large up-front capital investments to enter new markets and develop new products. It also enables companies to protect their operating cash flow because expenses rise when business volume rises, and decline when business volume declines. Companies can also easily exit unprofitable markets because they do not have to write off large capital investments and related sunk costs.

Driver for Variable Cost in a Cloud Solution

The major driver for organizations to adopt the variable cost model is the cloud's ability to create an agile and responsive system that responds to the changing market conditions and customer desires, while still being able to deliver profits.

The dynamic infrastructure implementation and enhanced utilization of IT assets in a cloud environment are the other driving forces for an organization to adopt a variable cost model of cloud computing.

Smart Meter for Checking on Usage of Cloud Infrastructure

The smart metering of cloud services prevents the wastage of computing power in low load conditions, and improves the overall utilization of cloud infrastructure. A mapping is derived between load condition in the cloud environment for a particular time period, and the standard pricing. The load condition in the cloud environment is predicted using the *ARIMA* statistical model, and monitoring of the cloud infrastructure is performed using *Hyperic*. The pricing information which is obtained as a function of load condition is produced as bill to the customer.

Time to Market

Cloud services provide rapid access to IT infrastructure, storage, and virtual server environments. Cloud services provide dynamic IT resource provisioning, where platforms are available that enable an organization to rapidly develop, deploy, manage, and integrate the applications that they develop. Therefore, cloud services reduce the average time to create and deploy a new solution, and also cut down on the engineering effort to deploy the solution. This in turn results in shorter times to market, thereby providing an organization with more time to create value in the organization.

Drivers for Time Required to Develop Software or Applications

Software development is a highly resource and budget intensive operation for a software organization. The business of the software organization is dramatically impacted by the timely delivery of applications. Cloud services streamline the delivery of applications, thereby enabling the speed of time to market. The important factors that drive the development of applications in a cloud environment are:

- The resources of the data center are provisioned through self-service access in an agile manner within a short span of time.

- The requirements for the application lifecycle are addressed in a wide range with the availability of multiple service levels.

- Usage-based billing during the expansion or contraction of the resources is done in a faster way.

- Multi-tier application architectures and virtual environments are supported.

- The migration of existing virtual server images and workloads into the cloud can be easily done.

Distribution over the Internet

Cloud services consist of infinite computing resources available on demand and delivered via the Internet. The cloud can be accessed at any time, by any user, and from any place. This facilitates a user to have reliable, scalable, virtualized, location independent, cost effective, and ubiquitous access to the cloud. However clouds, to a certain extent, maintain a basic threshold on reliability, privacy protection, access and usage rights, data security, and liability for loss or violation of data.

ACTIVITY 2-4

Understanding the Impact of Cloud Computing on Business

Scenario:

In this activity, you will review your knowledge of cloud computing and its impact on business.

---

1. **At which level does an organization benefit through the availability of elastic computing resources and pay-per-use models of cloud computing?**

   a) Utility

   b) Process Transformation

   c) Business Model Innovation

   d) Smart Metering

---

2. **What are the elements of an organization that are deployed at the Utility level? (Choose all that apply.)**

   a) Labor

   b) Software

   c) Hardware

   d) Business Model

Lesson 2 Follow-up

In this lesson, you analyzed the business aspects of cloud computing. You also identified various characteristics of cloud computing and its impact. With this knowledge, you will be able to identify the cloud technology that optimally meets your business and IT needs.

1. **What are the types of organizations that would benefit by migrating to cloud computing? In what category would you put your own organization?**

2. **What level of value provided by cloud computing would be most beneficial to your organization?**

3 | Technical Perspectives of Cloud Computing

Lesson Time: 2 hour(s)

Lesson Objectives:

In this lesson, you will differentiate the types of cloud solutions and the adoption measures needed for each.

You will:

● Define the cloud deployment methods.

● Identify the network requirements essential to deploy cloud services.

● Define automation and self-service.

● Identify the key characteristics of federation.

● Define the scope for standardization in cloud services.

Introduction

You are well aware of the impact of cloud computing on IT organizations on a business perspective. As the next step, you may now want to deploy one or more types of cloud services in your organization. In this lesson, you will learn how to integrate cloud services within your organization.

Cloud computing is not a "one size-fits all" solution. There are different categories of cloud services to suit your specific organizational requirements. Therefore, it needs to be customized and deployed keeping in mind the core business drivers. But how do we go about this seemingly tedious process? Knowing the different types of cloud services and understanding the processes used to deploy them are the first step.

TOPIC A
The Cloud Deployment Models

You are well aware of the various services offered by cloud computing and the impact it may have on business. You will need to identify the various types of cloud deployments that are available, to enable you to deploy your preferred service. In this topic, you will identify the various categories of cloud models.

Since every business has critical data and unique operational needs, it is essential for you to understand the pros and cons of every cloud model. Other factors that may influence your decision include business needs, financial capability, and security. Depending on the sensitivity of data, you want to choose a specific type of cloud service for the required level of access.

Public Cloud

Definition:

A *public cloud* is a cloud solution that provides dynamically provisioned resources on a self-service basis to customers via the Internet. Public cloud services are shared among many organizations, and may be free or offered on a pay-per-usage model. The public cloud is a standard computing model which is made available to the public through off-site service providers, such as Google, Salesforce.com, and Amazon. The users of public cloud services cannot gain control over the hosted computing infrastructure as the service providers are not in their vicinity.

Organizations using public cloud services eliminate the need to have the infrastructure, as the service providers provide the network, operating systems, servers, and storage space to the users. Also, users are allowed to access and use the software running on the service provider's environment, thus enabling multiple users to use the software from a centralized location.

Example:

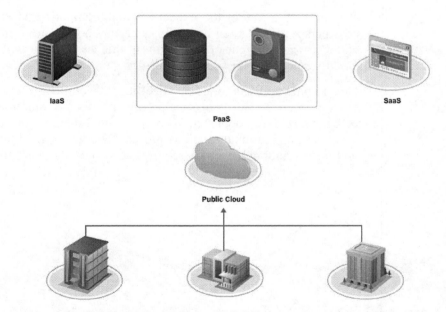

Figure 3-1: In a public cloud, resources are available through a third-party service provider.

Private Cloud

Definition:

A *private cloud* is a dedicated computing infrastructure owned and shared among users within the organization. The organizations adopting the private cloud services reap the benefits of owning their data centers, managing and monitoring data, load balancing, increased fault tolerance levels, backups, on-demand self-service, elasticity, and metered billing. Larger organizations build private clouds because they have special considerations around data protection or because their performance requirements necessitate tight control on the infrastructure.

Reasons for Private Cloud

The main reason for adopting private cloud services is to include the LDAP services or Active Directory into the cloud security system to authenticate the users' access. Having a private cloud enables the cloud administrator to automatically manage the user groups and provide role-based permission to users for access to cloud information.

Types of Private Cloud

There are two types of private cloud:

- On-premise private cloud – The hosted cloud services are managed and maintained by the organization itself.

- External private cloud – The hosted cloud services are managed by third party vendors but are exclusively used only by one organization.

Example:

Consider the example of an important government organization which has very specific requirements. Because of the large amount of computing resources they use, it makes sense for them to build a private cloud instead of risking their critical information in a public cloud. The private cloud implementation can still outsource the service but the infrastructure is set up in such a way that the private cloud is limited to a specific customer.

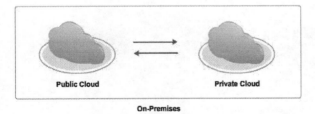

Figure 3-2: *In a private cloud, resources are maintained on-site.*

Hybrid Cloud

Definition:

A *hybrid cloud* is a combined application of both public and private cloud services whereby the organization stores their critical data in-house and moves the rest of the data to the cloud. The security norms of a private cloud combined with the efficiency of a public cloud can be availed together by the hybrid cloud users. Amazon's Virtual Private Cloud (VPC) is one of the leading examples of a hybrid cloud. VPC lets an organization securely connect its existing data center infrastructure to an isolated set of computer resources within the Amazon Web Services (AWS).

Cloud Bursting

Cloud bursting is an approach whereby an organization chooses not to invest in procuring hardware because they have reached the maximum provisioning capabilities, or because they use their infrastructure for normal usage and use cloud services only to manage high load requirements. In such cases, the organization will use additional hardware resources from the cloud vendors and pay for the usage of such resources.

Example:

OGC Solutions, an organization providing worldwide banking services, has to handle a wide range of data, most of which pertains to customer accounts. If this data is accessed by unauthorized users, it would jeopardize customer financial data. Therefore, the company decided to retain the customer accounts information on its own private cloud, and move the rest of the data to a public cloud, thereby benefitting from both services.

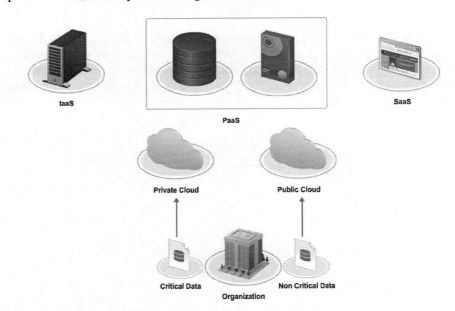

Figure 3-3: A hybrid cloud supporting various cloud applications.

Community Cloud

Definition:

A *community cloud* is a cloud solution in which organizations having common security practices and mission share hosted computing services. However, there might be several challenges associated with this type of sharing between organizations. Managing availability, service levels, and security across this community cloud might prove to be difficult.

Example:

For example, all government organizations within a state may share their computing infrastructure on the cloud to manage data related to citizens residing there. For this, they may subscribe to a single cloud provider for a similar service. In the community cloud, businesses with the same needs share computing resources.

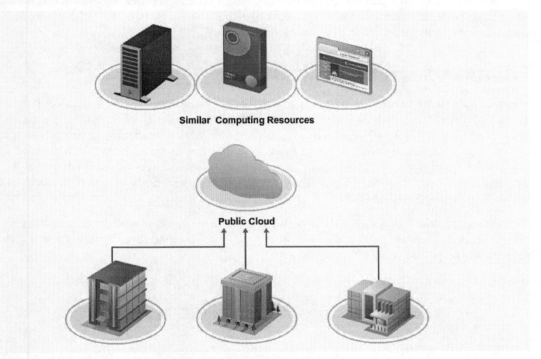

Figure 3-4: A community cloud is accessed by multiple organizations.

Public vs. Private Cloud

As there are technical differences between public and private clouds, choose the one which is most suitable for your organization. Organizations adopting public cloud services reap the advantages of instant provisioning, eliminating downtime, reduced cost of installation of hardware, eliminating the need to upgrade software, and minimal network problems. The major concerns to adopting public cloud services include data security, accountability, backups, and vendor lock-in.

Private cloud services enable the organization to provide maximum data security by maintaining firewalls, adhering to strict compliance measures, supervising access to data, providing for backups, and by load balancing. The major concerns in adopting private cloud services include the cost of maintenance, limited provisioning capabilities, and network outage problems.

Public vs. Community Cloud

There is a line of demarcation between the public cloud and a community cloud. Any user can procure the services of a public cloud for free, or on the on-demand basis. Organizations with common objectives, specific security policies, and compliance factors opt for community cloud services. A community cloud is partially a public cloud. This is because community cloud services are extended to organizations within that particular community. Users of community cloud services have the advantage of maximizing their productivity because only a particular type of organization uses the services.

The data security and adherence to compliance standards are dominant factors of a community cloud. As in the case of a public cloud, the concern that any user can use the services of the cloud on a pay and use basis threatens data security, compliance factors, and backup of data in the event of data loss. Also, public cloud providers are not necessarily in the vicinity of users. They may even be third party vendors from different locations whereas community cloud providers may be located on premises. The cost of using the services of a public cloud is comparatively lower than a community cloud.

Private vs. Hybrid Cloud

Organizations using private cloud services may either maintain their own data centers, or obtain the services from third party vendors. Hybrid cloud is a combination of public cloud and private cloud, wherein organizations can maintain vital information in the private cloud and migrate less critical information to the public cloud. Data portability is an assured factor of a hybrid cloud. Organizations using hybrid cloud services have the dual advantage of in sourcing and outsourcing data where they can develop applications in a public cloud, and then launch it in their private cloud.

The other advantages of using hybrid cloud services are scalability of data, capability of moving applications requiring peak load balancing to a public cloud, and avoiding the heavy cost incurred in the purchase of infrastructure.

ACTIVITY 3-1
Understanding the Categories of Cloud Computing

Scenario:

In this activity, you will review your knowledge of the categories of cloud computing.

1. **Which deployment model provides cloud services to a limited number of people within an organization?**

    a) Public cloud service

    b) Private cloud service

    c) Community cloud service

    d) Hybrid cloud service

2. **True or False? When costs are being shared among fewer users, public cloud computing is a more expensive venture.**

    ___ True

    ___ False

TOPIC B

Network Requirements for Cloud Deployment

You have identified the different cloud categories. You may now want to determine the various methods and techniques for deploying the appropriate cloud service. In this topic, you will identify the specific network requirements, the network topologies and key components of a cloud network which suit the requirements of your organizations

Having identified the different types of cloud deployment models, you may want to ascertain networking techniques to deploy cloud services. Choosing the appropriate network model will enable you to quicken response time, provide hardware resources dynamically and improve information management.

Cloud Networking Models

Most organizations strive to enhance scalability and maximize productivity with minimal investment in cloud network infrastructure and application. Earlier network models used a silo based approach where data centers consisted of the hardware setup, the applications, and the network residing in the same location. The advent of virtualization has improved IT strategies and has benefited organizations because virtualization creates replicas of infrastructure, applications, servers, and network resources.

With virtualization, a single application can be hosted on multiple machines, thus minimizing the need for repeated software installation. Also, hardware equipment can be divided into virtual networks, enabling the central IT resources to be available to all the departments in the organization via local networks.

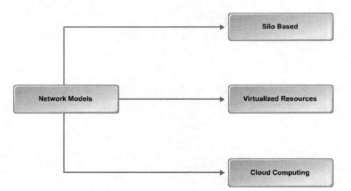

Figure 3-5: Three networking models.

The concept of a cloud is an extension of virtualization and drives networking models because virtualized IT resources, such as infrastructure, applications, network, servers, and operating systems can be acquired via the Internet on a demand and usage basis. Cloud providers possess the resources and charge consumers according to the usage. Cloud computing is location independent and can reside in any geographic location, still rendering the best services to users.

Cloud Network

Cloud data centers maintain multiple servers and store huge volumes of data. It is essential to provide sufficient network fabric suitable to support such an infrastructure. The cloud network should be designed to provide maximum throughput and data resilience so that free movement of resources between servers and data centers can be accomplished. The cloud network enables pairing of the network set up with the computing systems, and web applications.

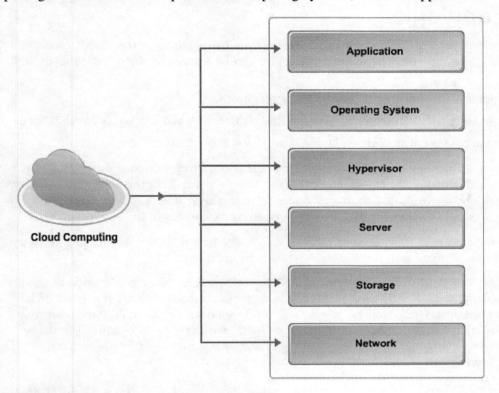

Figure 3-6: *Components of a cloud network.*

There are various components in a cloud network.

Components	Description
Application	Maximized access to applications using the scheduler. Examples include web applications, SaaS, PaaS and internal applications.
Operating System	A software application used in a computing system to manage the hardware components. Examples include any version of Windows, Solaris, and Linux
Hypervisor	Used to dissociate the applications and OS from the hardware. Examples include XVM, Hyper-V, ESX, and KVM.
Server	Used to minimize the administration cost of servers. Examples include bare-metal stateless servers.
Storage	File storage is attached to the network and no separate SAN is required.

Components	Description
Network	Delegates dynamic provisioning of servers, configuration set up and application deployment. Examples include CloudVision.

Cloud Topologies

The cloud topology depicts the manner in which the user gains access to the cloud resources via the network infrastructure. The cloud architecture can be viewed as three independent structures:

1. The front-end – It connects the user to the applications.
2. The horizontal aspect – It interconnects the different servers and storage network devices.
3. The larger network – It is built on layer 2 and layer 3 topologies.

The Open Systems Interconnection model (OSI model) is used to group the communication function into a series of logical layers. Each layer in this model is designed to provide services to the layer residing above it, and receive services from the layer below it. The Data Link Layer (Layer 2) is used to transfer data between the network entities in the cloud.

The Network Layer (Layer 3) is used to transfer data sequences with variable lengths from a source host of one network to a destination host of a different network.

In the larger network, a layer 2 cloud topology is more easily managed than layer 3. In a layer 3 network topology, each cloud is represented as a separate network with a defined set of IP addresses and attributes. Organizations adopting layer 3 cloud services should have their internal applications and services updated to match the cloud provider's requirements. The major concerns are re-designing and re-configuring the organization's network to suit the requirements of the cloud service provider.

The layer 2 network is not location dependent as it maintains the IP and MAC addresses to ensure that all the servers have the same addresses and routing protocols. In a layer 2 network, the network of the cloud is a direct prolongation of the network in the data center. There is no need for customers to re-design or re-configure their settings; they are at liberty to run their applications in the cloud or locally.

Virtual eXtensible LAN (VXLAN)

VXLAN is a segmentation mechanism that enables the deployment of virtual machines in any server in the network. IT organizations using VXLAN can create a scalable network architecture to support the addition of machines on demand, irrespective of the location factors and IP address.

Key Characteristics of Cloud Networks

Cloud networks have a few distinct characteristics.

Characteristics	Description
Scalability of performance	Scalability makes IT management simpler because a significant portion of your resources reside on the cloud and are managed by the cloud provider. Also, the cloud network infrastructure should ensure that maximum throughput is handled and quick service is provided to the applications in the network, thus guaranteeing increased performance levels.
Resiliency	The downtime for cloud services should be minimal as the network infrastructure offers self-remedial measures.
Latency	The response time to render the services should be in microseconds to improve the performance of the application and maximize utilization of servers.
Extended Management	An approach to handle the automatic provisioning, monitoring, upgrading and maintenance of network resources.

Potential Problem Areas in a Cloud Network

The cloud operates on several thousands of servers to deliver services and resources to customers. Cloud service providers should optimize network latencies to promote quicker response times. There are key areas of concerns associated with network latency.

Type	Description
Network node latency	It is essential to reduce the latency of each network node to improve its performance levels. The use of optimized fabric in the cloud network architecture will serve in minimizing transport latency levels.
Number of nodes traversed for each stage	A three tier architecture consisting of servers, distribution, and core switch layers maximizes the number of hops required for the traversal of data packets. In order to reduce the latency, cloud service providers can adopt a two-tier topology so that data packets will traverse fewer hops.
Network congestion	Data packets are transported by Transmission Control Protocol (TCP). In the event of network congestion, TCP uses smaller windows which pose a threat to data reliability and throughput. This problem can be avoided by using congestion-free fabric to design the network architecture, thus enabling TCP to use large windows for low latency and high throughput.
Transport protocol latency	To reap the benefits of no data loss, super low latency levels, and efficient throughput, cloud providers can use ethernet fabric to design the network architecture so that performance is maximized, performance levels and the risk of network congestion is eliminated.

Content Delivery Network (CDN)

CDN is a caching mechanism which stores the data from the original server in multiple nodes on the network. The customer can retrieve information from these cached nodes instead of the original server, thus reducing the number of network hops required to obtain data. CDN increases the access bandwidth and reduces access latency.

ACTIVITY 3-2

Identifying the network requirements for Cloud Deployment

Scenario:

In this activity, you will review your knowledge on the network requirements of cloud computing.

1. **What are the essential components of a cloud network? (Choose all that apply.)**

   a) Scalability

   b) Hypervisor

   c) Latency

   d) Storage

   e) Operating System

2. **True or False? Network node latency can be reduced by using optimized fabric.**

   ___ True

   ___ False

TOPIC C
Automation and Self-Service in Cloud Computing

You have reviewed the various network requirements for adopting cloud services. The next step is to go ahead and identify the techniques to deploy cloud services. To do this, you need to rapidly deploy your services using automation techniques and provide suitable measures to authenticate people to use the cloud services. In this topic, you will identify factors that contribute to effective implementation of automation and elements of self-service.

There is one critical question lost in the hype surrounding cloud computing: "How do you get there?" Sure, you'd like to reap the benefit of cloud computing, such as reduced costs, operational efficiency, and application flexibility. However, you might be worried about the process of migrating to cloud services. Automation enables you to reduce the time taken to provision the servers to transform to the cloud. Self-service authorizes a user to receive the appropriate cloud services.

Automation of Operations in Cloud Computing

The need to provide improved IT services is a driving force for organizations to manage complex infrastructure and control the cost of acquiring associated resources. It is important for organizations to maintain an automation solution to provide controlled and secured access to your applications and hardware resources.

The advent of cloud computing proved to be advantageous for automating the provisioning and scheduling of hardware resources (virtual machines) to cater to the needs of customers. The automation services rendered by cloud service providers include:

- The task of managing and provisioning the infrastructure (IaaS), such as servers, the network, database, and storage, while centralizing the norms for security and usage.
- The scope for multi-tenancy (SaaS), which is an added advantage, whereby multiple organizations can not only access an instance of software residing on a server, but also access databases, and packaged applications.
- A highly flexible architecture with advanced workload optimization and metering, service assurance, application lifecycle management, security, and compliance.

Attributes of Effective Automation

Automated cloud services have three key attributes.

Attributes	Description
Resource Pool	- Identify the unused infrastructure in the resource pool and utilize the same for provisioning. - Organize the physical storage servers into a resource pool based on their performance, capacity, location, and cost.

Attributes	Description
Provisioning Attributes	• Determine the type of storage, depending on the provisioning policy. • The ability for a provisioning protocol to automatically resize the volume of data when the storage container reaches the maximum threshold.
Data Protection	• Protection standards for recovery of data in the event of network outages, system failures, and operating errors. • Standards for data backup, and recovery plans.

Benefits of Automation

The organizational benefits of automated cloud services include:

• Optimized utilization of resources on a demand basis, regardless of the physical location of the cloud vendor.

• Provisioning of servers, and disaster recovery plans and the ability to handle complex infrastructure operations.

• Improved response time and reduced risk of server downtime.

• Adherence to strict compliance standards to obtain assured quality services, and development and delivery of new services.

• And, minimized cost of power consumption for hardware resources.

Customer Self-Service

Customer self-service is a key component of cloud computing as it allows consumers to request cloud services and authenticate, and use appropriate services from the virtualized resource pool. Users can reap greater benefits by maximizing hardware and resource utilization and improved scalability. To improve productivity, users with appropriate permissions can automate repetitive activities such as creating email IDs for new users.

CAPTCHA

Completely Automated Public Turing test to tell Computers and Humans Apart (CAPTCHA) is a program which generates and grades tests to ensure that the response is created by a human and not another computer. CAPTCHA plays a significant role in self-service as it dismisses hackers from accessing websites by asking for authentication. Another concept of CAPTCHA is the Turing Test which measures the intelligence of a machine. For instance, if a conversation is held between a human and a computer, a third person should not be able to distinguish the response of the computer from that of the human.

Challenges to Automation and Self-Service

Organizations may refrain from deploying cloud services, for reasons such as:

- Data security and reliability – Cloud services are extended to users via the Internet. The data may be more vulnerable to hackers. It is essential for the cloud vendors to adopt security and compliance standards, and guarantee the security of data.

- Compatibility – The transformation of complex data and infrastructure into the cloud is another serious concern as it might not be compatible with the cloud technology, or it may be too complex to be restructured.

ACTIVITY 3-3

Identifying the Techniques of Automation and Self-service in Cloud Computing

Scenario:

In this activity, you will review your knowledge on the automation and self-service techniques of cloud computing.

1. **What are the key benefits of cloud automation? (Choose all that apply.)**

   a) Optimal utilization of the cloud resources

   b) Minimal cost incurred for maintenance (power consumption)

   c) High operating costs

   d) Adherence to compliance standards for data security

2. **True or False? User authentication is the basic attribute of self-service.**

   ___ True

   ___ False

TOPIC D
Federated Cloud Services

You are familiar with the automation technique and the elements of self-service. As the next step, you will explore ways of maximizing utilization of resources, without the need to re-configure or re-build your network capabilities. In this topic, you will identify the key characteristics of federated cloud services.

The use of automation and self-service techniques provides resources and access to information by privileged users. Similarly, the use of federated cloud services permits organizations to easily implement the transformation process without the implementation of a major change in network design.

Federation Cloud Services

As a general term, federation is the integration of smaller parts to perform a range of common actions. As related to cloud technology, federation is a technique used by a cloud service provider to purchase or rent infrastructure, or applications from another provider for meeting excessive consumer demand and load balancing. Additionally, providers can maximize resource utilization by expanding their services across geographic boundaries without the need to deploy computing resources worldwide.

For the consumers of services, cloud federation is an added advantage as abundant services are available in a federated cloud, the cost is low, the performance of web applications is better, and there is a reduction in vendor lock-in.

Internal Data Center

The use of an internal data center can put restraints on users because of limitations on physical storage space, consumption of power, and a heavy investment in maintenance, operation cost, and network issues. CloudSwitch is a software solution which bridges the services of an internal data center to the cloud without imposing major modifications in the workload and network setup. CloudSwitch ensures data security by adapting encryption and isolation standards. It also enables the integration of applications to the data center tools and policy norms, and the movement of applications between different cloud environments and back into the data center.

Federation Benefits

The benefits offered through cloud federation are:

* Increased availability of resources.
* Relocation of unused resources from one service provider to another to enable maximum resource utilization.
* Availability of multiple copies of data in different storage locations, providing users with quick access to information.
* Minimizing of vendor lock-in issues, as replicated data is available on many servers.
* Better availability of resources as network related problems will not be a hindrance.
* And, assurance of lower costs and high performance levels.

Security in a Federated Environment

In a federated cloud environment where the exchange of information is applicable between the internal data center and the cloud, security and compliance standards are a major concern. Key security concerns include the audit policies followed by the cloud service providers, the physical location of data, and the security norms adopted by providers to ensure data protection. Cloud service providers incorporate their solution to security concerns in the Service Level Agreement (SLA).

Security assurance is based on the different cloud service models.

Cloud Service Models	Security Measures
Software as a Service (SaaS)	This model focuses on managing access to applications. Service providers should establish a control mechanism to authenticate the privileges that users have, to access the applications. Consider the case where there are thousands of employees accessing cloud applications. It is not practical to create passwords for each employee. Instead, service providers can create a single sign-on mechanism for users to access both, online premises and applications in the cloud.
Platform as a Service (PaaS)	In PaaS, the vital point to be considered is data protection, because data loss is more prevalent in this model due to network outage issues. Service providers should assure data security by adopting load balancing techniques and encryption standards.
Infrastructure as a Service (IaaS)	In this model, it is essential for the providers of federated cloud services to define in the SLA, the details about the network topology, the creation of virtual machines, and the pattern in which they are spun down to avoid wastage of resources and uncontrolled access.

Encryption Standards

In a federated cloud environment, user benefits include low cost of resource utilization and agility. The major concern is securing data and resources in the cloud. The problem of data security can be eradicated by applying encryption and compliance standards. From the customer's perspective, users are authenticated by the usage of passwords, encryption standards and digital certificates. The providers use encryption standards such as Advanced Encryption Standards and 3-Data Encryption Standards (3DES) to ensure that data protection is the highest priority in rendering cloud services.

Cloud Storage Gateway

Cloud storage services are essential for data backup and archiving. Organizations adopting the services of cloud storage should analyze the risk involved in the security, performance and availability of data. To overcome the barriers of cloud storage, organizations are switching to the cloud storage gateway network. The cloud storage gateway is a server residing in the customers' premises to ensure data protection by encrypting backup, data compression, data recovery, and archiving data sets before the transformation to cloud. Additionally, the cloud storage gateway eliminates the issue of vendor lock-in because it supports backup of applications and storage.

Characteristics of Cloud Gateway

Cloud gateway has a few distinct characteristics.

Characteristics	Description
Data backup	The protection of data against the occurrence of any data loss event is very essential. The backup mechanism propagates the need to replicate data to instigate the need for recovery on account of loss or corruption of data.
Cloud cache	Caching is the buffering of vital data to speed up the process of information retrieval, instead of fetching the data from the original server.
Data encryption	The process of transforming data into an unreadable format to protect the data from being accessed by unprivileged users or hackers.
Provisioning of network resources	Spawning of new instances of machines in the network to enable organizations to utilize the services of the cloud.
Data compression	The compression algorithms are used to compress data in order to minimize the consumption of resources such as the network bandwidth, and hardware space in the cloud.

Identity Management for Federation

Organizations widely use many applications from the cloud via the Internet. Authentication of a valid user is the prime concern in this regard. Additionally, different applications from various service providers across the cloud require multiple levels of permissions. A unique identity system is essential to authenticate the user to access the applications.

In user identity management the mapping is one-to-many, or many-to-one or even pseudonyms. A pseudonym is a privacy protection, and is applied by a user to avoid the exposure of his identity when using the federated cloud.

Consider the example of purchasing a commodity via the Internet. The consumer will choose the supplier based on his requirements such as the price of the commodity when compared to other vendors, the time taken to ship the commodity, the shipment procedure followed by the supplier, etc. Finally, the transaction order reaches the supplier. The supplier approves the transaction and releases the commodity for shipping. In each step of this transaction, the federation authority exposes essential attributes of the customer to each department involved with the purchase of the commodity.

Federated ID Management by Sun

Sun Microsystems uses the Sun Java System Federation Manager for building the federated identity services between service providers and consumers. The use of identity standards such as SAML and the Liberty Alliance's ID-FF (Identity Federation Framework), enables the federation manager to link the identity of privileged users across applications in the cloud.

ACTIVITY 3-4
Identifying the Key Components of Federated Cloud Services

Scenario:

In this activity, you will review your knowledge on the key components of federated cloud services.

1. **True or False? The use of pseudonyms is not encouraged in user identity management systems of a federated cloud environment because it is a breach of trust.**

   ___ True

   ___ False

2. **What are the chief characteristics of the Cloud Gateway? (Choose all that apply.)**

   a) Data resiliency

   b) Data backup

   c) Cloud cache

   d) Provisioning of network resources

TOPIC E
Standardization

You now have an idea of the federated cloud services, what they comprise, and what kind of services the technology can offer. Since a federated cloud is exposed to multiple users spread over different geographic locations, various standards and compliance measures need to be adopted by the service providers to ensure the security of data. In this topic, you will identify the various standards and audit measures adopted by the consumers and service providers.

Having identified the benefits of using federated cloud services, it is essential to understand the standards and security norms adopted by the various cloud service providers of the intercloud community. Knowing the compliance standards adopted by the providers and the assurance they give for the security of the data in the cloud, will help you choose the appropriate provider, based on your requirements.

Interoperability

The key component of a federated cloud is the interoperability feature which effectively addresses the issues of vendor lock-in and furnishes the need for integration of service providers to extend better services. The interoperability feature enables users to utilize resources to the fullest extent as they are rendered by multiple integrated service providers, eliminating the restriction of geographic locations. On the other hand, the service providers use de-facto standards to offer distributed service to consumers. The use of cloud computing will be hampered in the absence of interoperable features to integrate data and applications.

Cloud Computing Standards

The trend for adopting cloud services has introduced new innovations, risk factors, and adoption policies which bring about the need to use standards as a critical element for the successful adoption of cloud strategies. There are different cloud computing standards adopted by service providers.

Types of Standards	Description
Cloud Security Alliance	This organization was started with the primary aim of adhering to security assurance standards to encourage best practices of cloud computing services. • Cloud Control Matrix – It was designed to provide the basic security principles to guide service providers and aid consumers in assessing the security risk involved in choosing a cloud provider. • Top Threats to Cloud Computing – It assists organizations in analyzing risk management factors in cloud adoption strategies. • Cloud Audit – It is a common interface for cloud providers to automate the assessment, and audit their infrastructure (IaaS), platform (PaaS), and applications (SaaS).
Cloud Standard Customer Council	Its main focus is to educate the end user about the cloud adoption measures, the security, and interoperability features during the course of transition to the cloud.

Types of Standards	Description
Distributed Management Task Force	An organization that was started to effectively launch standards to manage cloud interoperability between the consumers and service providers.
The Green Grid	An organization to create standards for the maximum utilization of cloud resources.
National Institute of Standards and Technology (NIST)	The NIST has created standards to govern cloud architecture, deployment strategies, and security of federated cloud services.

Standards for Private Cloud

The private cloud abides by the set of standards, mandatory to the organization it is associated with, such as the ISO standards and Infrastructure Library (ITIL). Additionally, the private cloud should adopt the standards for backup, security, documentation and SLA requirements.

Standards for Public Cloud

Public cloud adopts audit standards and compliance measures, such as SAS 70. Additionally, the Audit ISO 27001 certification for security management processes, and ISO 27002 controls for relevant subsets are in place.

Approaches to Implement Interoperability

Cloud providers have created a common forum called the Cloud Computing Interoperability Forum (CCIF), to address compliance issues, standardization techniques, and the problem of cloud interoperability. CCIF is planning to launch the unified cloud interface. The features of the unified cloud interface are:

● To merge all the cloud API's together and project them behind a standardized cloud interface.

● To provide a unified interface for the infrastructure stack and merge cloud-centric technologies.

● To serve as a common interface for interactions between network, applications, servers, systems, identity, and data.

● A common set of cloud definitions that cater to the exchange of management information across cloud providers spread over different geographic locations.

Alternative Approach

The other approach for cloud interoperability is the creation of an orchestration layer. Many organizations seek to increase the speed and adoption of their products by transforming their services to cloud. Since interoperability is the key component of cloud, it is essential to provide an orchestration mechanism to enhance the usage of these interclouds or federated cloud environments. Cloud Orchestration mechanism was initiated by a few cloud vendors such as Rightscale, Cordys, and Eli Lilly to design a single management platform to collate the services of federated cloud.

Compliance with Various Functional/Industry Standards

It is essential to implement a cloud solution standard that considers all the key requirements and establish specific remedies to challenges that can arise in a cloud environment. A set of standards and compliance measures is already in place to address the concerns around cloud computing. The industry norms and standards for compliance issues in cloud computing include:

- Industries like banking sectors, healthcare, and financial services follow the standards prescribed in the Personal Information Act which governs the protection of personal information of the consumers of the service.

- Country-wide compliance and security norms have also been implemented by defining the audit process and the regulatory measures for ensuring data privacy and access.

- Depending on the size of the company, the standards and compliance measures are defined in the SLA to describe the type of data being stored or processed.

ACTIVITY 3-5
Identifying the Standardization Norms Followed in Cloud Computing

Scenario:

In this activity, you will review your knowledge of the standards and compliance measures of cloud computing environment.

---

1. **True or False? Interoperability in federated cloud reduces the need for vendor lock-in.**

   ___ True

   ___ False

---

2. **What are the various standards adopted by the service providers to ensure the security of data in a federated cloud environment? (Choose all that apply.)**

   a) Cloud Security Alliance

   b) The Green Grid

   c) SAS 70

   d) Cloud Computing interoperability forum

Lesson 3 Follow-up

In this lesson, you investigated the various possible ways to integrate your organization's IT operations with the cloud. Identifying the different types of cloud, and the technical aspects to deploy cloud services will enable you to choose the cloud type suitable for your organization.

1. **Which cloud deployment model will you prefer for your organization?**

2. **What key characteristics of a federated cloud might attract your organization? Why?**

4 | Technical Challenges of Cloud Computing

Lesson Time: 2 hour(s)

Lesson Objectives:

In this lesson, you will identify the technical challenges and the mitigation measures involved in cloud computing.

You will:

● Describe the technical challenges in adopting cloud services.

● Describe the challenges related to application performance in cloud computing.

● Define the challenges faced when integrating data into the cloud.

● Describe the challenges of handling security issues when adopting to cloud services.

● Describe the application development process and architecture in cloud.

Introduction

While you know that adopting cloud computing services will be advantageous from the business and technical perspectives, a few questions have been raised about the technical challenges faced when deploying cloud services. In this lesson, you will get to know the possible technical hindrances to adapt to when using cloud computing and the ways to mitigate them.

Every industry faces varied levels of risks and challenges. Organizations offering financial services need to follow certain data practices; organizations undertaking software development face challenges associated with timely delivery of the product in the market; and healthcare organizations have challenges associated with maintaining patient privacy. Therefore, a company deploying cloud computing needs to be aware of the kinds of challenges it is likely to face and the ways to tackle them.

TOPIC A
Cloud Storage

You now have an idea of what kind of technical benefits you can acquire when you opt for cloud services. There is bound to be a flip-side to any new technology being implemented in your organization. Therefore, it is essential to identify the technical challenges you will face when you adopt cloud services. In this topic, you will identify the technical challenges associated with deploying a cloud computing service.

Cloud computing is an exciting technology, but any technology will have pros and cons. It involves risks, and the first step in preparing yourself to overcome such challenges is to identify the technical barriers involved in adopting cloud services.

Features of Cloud Storage

Over time, many big Internet based companies realized that only a small amount of their data storage capacity is being used. This unoptimized storage has led to the renting of storage space on a cloud. Cloud storage has seven primary features.

Feature	Description
Availability	A fault in one database system will affect only that fragment of information and not the entire database. Thus, cloud storage illustrates improved availability.
Performance	With cloud services, databases are parallelized and data is located near the site with the greatest demand. This ensures that load is balanced among servers resulting in high performance.
Price	A cloud is a network of smaller computers with the ability of larger ones, making it highly cost effective.
Flexibility	You can modify the storage features of the system without having to harm the entire database.
Complexity	Additional administrative work is required to maintain the system.
Security	Security is a critical factor because data on cloud is vulnerable to hackers.
Integrity	Maintaining integrity of the database is indeed a challenge if the database is too complex.

Data Redundancy

With increasing concurrent access of data on the cloud, data integrity and availability need to be maintained across an unreliable set of computers over a wide area network such as the Internet. Data retrieval efficiency is achieved through replication of data and services and distributing them across different resources to achieve load-balancing. The source node will add some level of redundancy to each data block. This redundancy allows the system to re-create the entire block even if some nodes are temporarily unavailable, due to loss of network connectivity, the machine being powered off, or a hardware failure. Implicitly, data consistency needs to be maintained over a wide distribution of replicated data sources. At the same time, the system always needs to be aware of the data location when replicating across data centers, taking latencies and particularly workload into consideration.

Redundancy as an Effective Disaster Recovery Plan

Redundant systems back up programs and files from a primary server onto a secondary server. Redundancy acts as an effective disaster recovery plan in several ways.

- It allows seamless transition if something happens to the primary server.
- It increases the overall productivity of employees with fewer downtimes.
- It ensures the complete restoration of the primary system faster than other data recovery options.

Challenges with Backup

There are several challenges concerning backup while deploying cloud services.

Challenge	Description
Bandwidth	Network bandwidth has to scale up or down depending upon the size of data residing on the cloud.
Security	Security is the most critical concern of any organization adopting cloud services even if the cloud vendor promises top-notch security.
Recovery	Recovery processes are tougher when your data resides on the cloud.

Data Replication

Data replication is a process of creating multiple copies of the enterprise's data in the cloud to instigate the need for data recovery on account of any data loss due to unexpected events. In the event of any problem in the enterprise's primary site, key application services can be restarted and run at the remote location until the primary site is brought back online. The features of cloud storage fits with data replication as the cost and complexity of disaster recovery are handled more efficiently.

Data Residency

When you move your data to the cloud, are you aware where exactly your data is being stored? Customer data is stored in various locations in the cloud, to ensure scalability and efficiency. An organization's data may not reside within the same country as their business. Additionally, the privacy laws vary drastically between countries and regions which restricts the access of data according to the laws enforced in that specific country or region. When deploying a cloud service, you need to know in which legal jurisdiction your data resides. But it is often difficult to determine this information, as your data is constantly in motion in the cloud.

Reliability

In most cloud computing environments, there is a trade-off between reliability and the speed of deployment. Reliability of cloud service is a critical factor but it is often too hard to analyze due to certain characteristics of cloud. Some of them are massive-scale sharing of services, wide-area network, heterogeneous software and hardware components and complicated interactions among them.

Disaster Recovery

Disaster recovery in cloud computing is one of the most important considerations for any customer when investigating service providers. Disaster recovery with cloud computing has several benefits.

Benefit	Description
Easy deployment	In cloud computing, virtual servers are created using virtualization technologies, making it easy to copy the entire virtual server including patches to a new server.
Rapid provisioning	Virtual servers are hardware independent, and so can be safely and accurately transferred from one data center to another. Virtual servers allow you to copy the entire environment and run it on another cloud environment.
Scalability	If more processing power is needed, then more CPUs and RAM can be allocated easily without any downtime.
Cost effective	Virtual servers provide fast recovery at minimal cost.

There are primarily five issues concerning disaster recovery with cloud services.

Issue	Description
Limited application support	Most cloud-based disaster recovery vendors provide infrastructure based on commodity Windows or Linux-based systems and databases. As a result, they may not be able to replicate data and update databases from older, non-web based applications without developing a customized system.
Insufficient bandwidth	Many cloud vendors provide just replication service instead of complete disaster recovery due to lack of bandwidth.
Financial considerations	Smaller companies prefer the idea of data backup services from cloud instead of having to maintain their own IT infrastructure. On the other hand, larger companies find it financially beneficial to build their own infrastructure.
Supplier issues	A gap between services provided and the customer expectations is bound to exist, because they do not have a clear idea of the dependencies between different application sets and middleware components.

Data Fragmentation

The breaking up of data in memory into many pieces is nothing but data fragmentation. Due to the fragmentation phenomenon, the storage space in a computer is used inefficiently, thus reducing the storage capacity and performance. If the cloud storage contains customer data, which is now off premise and being managed by the business, data fragmentation will be a major problem, thereby increasing the need for a comprehensive data management approach.

ACTIVITY 4-1
Describing Cloud Storage

Scenario:

In this activity, you will review your knowledge on cloud storage.

1. **Identify the challenges involved in cloud service backup. (Choose all that apply.)**

   a) Bandwidth

   b) Security

   c) Reliability

   d) Recovery

2. **True or False? In cloud computing, there is a trade-off between reliability and the speed of deployment.**

   ___ True

   ___ False

TOPIC B
Application Performance

You identified the challenges associated with cloud storage. Cloud-based applications are widely deployed to improve business, making it another critical part of cloud services. In this topic, you will identify the challenges related to cloud application performance.

In recent times, cloud applications, in the form of SaaS, have gained tremendous popularity among business users. This makes it inevitable to monitor and improve cloud application performance consistently to ensure business continuity.

Cloud Performance and the Network

Cloud performance refers to the performance of cloud servers in terms of processor, memory and storage use, and the performance of cloud-based applications. Cloud performance monitoring helps administrators track the widely varying workloads to which cloud applications are subjected, noting potential problems under peak loads. Application scalability and performance are assured factors of benefits in cloud computing, but the distances between the hardware resources in the cloud and their connectivity cannot be controlled, as services of the cloud are location independent. In cloud computing, bandwidth is not a limiting factor in most scenarios, but round trip latency is. The ability to control latency is very minimal as data is spread over geographic locations and so it is vital for consumers to thoroughly scrutinize the SLA for the assurance given by the vendors for improved latency.

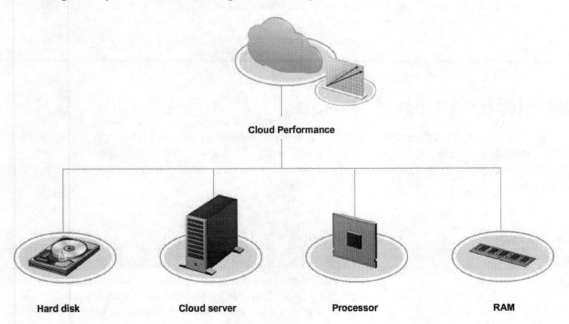

Figure 4-1: *Different resources contributing to cloud performance.*

 Round trip latency refers to the time delay experienced when data moves from source location to the destination and back to source.

Stability of the Cloud

Cloud computing performance is not always stable. Multi-tenancy is the key component of cloud instability, whereby multiple users access the resources (storage, processor, network, and memory) of the cloud simultaneously.

The challenges faced in cloud when determining stability of services are unique to each type of service.

Cloud Types	Description
SaaS	The increase in the number of software licenses issued by vendors to consumers prompts the issue of over usage of the software by multiple users. This might lead to performance and security issues of data in cloud.
PaaS	The challenges faced in offering stable PaaS services are: • Cost of performance • Load balancing • Database management • Adequate training of personnel to gain exposure of the different applications available in cloud and use specific applications to derive the estimated output.
IaaS	The stability of IaaS services offered by cloud are subject to some challenges: • Highly dependent on the Internet, so prone to outage issues. • Exposure of critical information to vendors and more possibilities of vendor lock-in. • User privacy and customizations options are highly curtailed in IaaS.

Monitoring Cloud Usage

It is essential that an organization monitor the way employees use cloud computing systems to ensure that they derive all the benefits of the service. To address the requirement of every cloud service, the monitoring system should be able to face the challenges unique to each type of service.

Cloud Types	Description
SaaS	• Multi-tenant – Since cloud uses a single instance of an application to cater to the needs of many users, monitoring, and profiling individual client performance is a difficult task. It is vital to monitor the performance issues specific to a tenant and also the integrity of the software. • Application end to end latency – Since the usage of cloud services is location independent, it is difficult to monitor the effective application response time, as the response time could be slow due to the Internet or overusage of the application.

Cloud Types	Description
PaaS	Gaining an insight on the client side processing of information is not possible and the monitoring tools have several restrictions in this area.
IaaS	• Virtualized Resource Pool – Monitoring individual physical nodes connected via the network can be eliminated and the use of virtualization to control and monitor the computing resources and storage implemented.
	• Load Testing – The network traffic in cloud is unpredictable as the usage is unlimited. So, load testing and monitoring the traffic is a tedious task.

Performance Management for Cloud-Hosted Applications

The cloud uses virtualized applications, and so it is essential to assess the performance of the application from the customer perspective such as:

• Identifying and resolving application performance problems.

• The response time required to use an application in cloud, since the location is not a constraint in cloud.

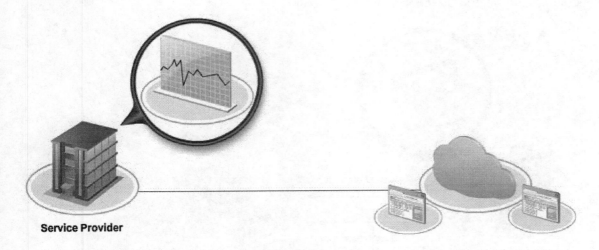

Service Provider

Figure 4-2: Measuring the performance of the virtual applications residing in the cloud

Performance Management Challenge	Description
Monitoring servers	You cannot effectively monitor and maintain the cloud-based infrastructure if you are unaware of how applications are interacting with their virtual servers.

Performance Management Challenge	Description
Choosing APM tools	Application Performance Management (APM) tools enable you to take maximum advantage of cloud service features such as elasticity and scalability. Choosing and deploying the appropriate APM tool is often a challenge.
Monitoring OS	Everything, even in the cloud, runs on operating systems. So, it is essential that you understand that OS processes completely unrelated to your hosted application can scuttle its performance and ruin your end-users' experience.
Installing OS patches and updates	Installing the patches and updates of operating systems is absolutely essential to ensure system stability and security.
Monitoring databases	Databases are as important as the operating system when you deploy a cloud service. Databases, when not maintained and optimized, can affect application performance dramatically.

Application Response Time

Application response time is the interval between a user-command and the receipt of an action from the application. Since resource utilization is not a reliable indicator of application performance in virtualized and cloud based environments, the focus needs to shift to response time as the primary metric of applications' performance.

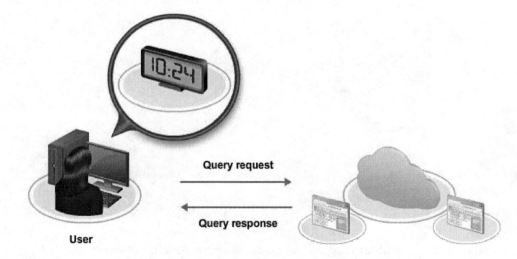

Figure 4-3: Gauging the response time for a query in the cloud.

By understanding the application response time, users can determine whether the cloud applications meet their service delivery commitments.

Server Memory Usage

Cloud computing puts considerable pressure on server memory for several reasons. Elasticity services of cloud computing rely on distribution of jobs and pooling of resources.

Challenge	Description
Server storage space	The storage space of the server may not be utilized completely, thus resulting in the lack of continuous flow of operations.
Cost saving	Consumers may tend to use a cost saving mechanism by using limited amount of servers, thus resulting in adding more pressure to fewer machines, and degrading services.
Elasticity	Jobs need to be partitioned into smaller tasks and distributed across many servers that have enough on-board memory to perform their respective tasks.
More memory space	• Cloud computing deploys browser-based thin client architecture, which shifted the memory requirements toward the server. The multi-tenancy feature of cloud computing demands massive amounts of memory due to CPU virtualization. • Applications related to database such as transactional database applications and web productivity applications require huge memory, due to CPU virtualization.

Memory Leaks

A memory leak is a situation in which a program, an application, or a part of the operating system does not return the memory allocated for temporary use though the memory is no longer in use. This can result in gradual loss of memory or inability of the program or application to function. A few operating systems have leak detection systems to identify the leak before the application crashes.

Improving Cloud Database Performance

Many cloud computing platforms are adding or enhancing their database offerings, thus becoming more compelling to enterprises. Cloud databases can offer significant advantages over their traditional counterparts, including increased accessibility, fast disaster recovery from failures, automated scalability, and minimal investment and maintenance of in-house hardware.

On the other hand, cloud databases have their own drawbacks, such as security and privacy issues. Sometimes, cloud databases can suffer from the inability to retrieve critical data in the event of a disaster or bankruptcy of the cloud service provider.

ACTIVITY 4-2
Describing Application Performance

Scenario:

In this activity, you will review your knowledge on application performance on cloud.

---

1. **Identify the challenges involved in performance management of cloud applications. (Choose all that apply.)**

   a) Monitoring operating systems

   b) Monitoring databases

   c) Monitoring servers

   d) Monitoring usage

---

2. **Identify the benefits of cloud databases. (Choose Three)**

   a) Improved security

   b) Increased accessibility

   c) Automated scalability

   d) Minimal investment

TOPIC C
Data Integration

You identified the challenges associated with application performance within the cloud. With data scattered in different locations, data integration becomes critical with cloud services. To be able to integrate data, you need to identify the challenges associated with it. In this topic, you will identify the challenges faced when you implement data integration in the cloud.

Data is located in numerous locations, and the pace of change has increased radically and our ability to control it has diminished. All these factors make cloud integration inevitable, which in turn demands awareness of the challenges you might face with data integration in the cloud.

Data Integration

Data resides in different locations on the cloud and so integrating it to provide users with a unified view of data becomes critical. There are several challenges involved in data integration over the cloud.

Challenge	Description
Data distribution	Data can be widely distributed. As a result, there are as many mainframes running today as in a traditional database system.
Speed of change	Faster changes are the toughest challenge for data integration. Because, once integration is complete, everything changes.
Distributed control	It is impossible to deny that the control over data is greatly reduced with the advent of cloud computing. This is because the control of the infrastructure and service has shifted from IT people and vendors to customers in different locations.
Connectivity	With almost every type of service moving to the cloud, connectivity is becoming a bigger challenge. Because if you lose connectivity, you lose the data, your time, and your work.
Data volumes	With an unimaginable rate of increase, data volume is ever expanding. Integrators need to increase their ability to handle data load as the data volume increases.

Data Synchronization

Data synchronization is the process of establishing consistency among data from a source to the target and vice versa. It establishes data harmony over time as data changes. With unsynchronized data, neither the cloud provider nor consumers will be able to understand each other's needs. With data synchronization, both of them work on identical information and therefore eliminate confusion.

Data Transformation

Data transformation is the conversion of information or data from one format to another, thus enabling the usage of data by multiple applications. The process involves three key challenges.

Challenge	Description
Run-time environment	Not all transformation processes are compatible with every run-time environment.
Data redundancy	When you implement the data transformation process over cloud, there is a possibility of redundant data.
Implementation cost	The implementation costs can be quite high at times when the process is not automated.

Data Migration

Cloud computing offers a convenient way to migrate data from legacy systems to a cloud. Migration is more agile and responsive than the traditional methods. But inevitably, there are several challenges associated with data migration to the cloud.

Challenge	Description
Data protection	Compliance with data protection legislation is a key to organizations where critical data is involved.
Data interruption	The cloud and underlying Internet infrastructure mean that there could be data flow interruptions.
Liability implications	Liability is a contentious issue in contracts. Depending upon the data being migrated and the value of the contract, service providers will try to limit their liability by reference to the value of the contract.

Security and Compliance Needs

It is the responsibility of the service provider to provide assurance to an organization about the security of their data in the cloud. There are a lot of compliance standards and audit procedures followed by the service provider to ensure the security of the data, applications, and hardware resources residing in the cloud. It is the responsibility of the consumer to conduct periodic audits trails to ensure the security of their application residing in the cloud.

Regardless of the kind of compliance standards that must be followed, the cloud provider is responsible for maintaining the security of the physical infrastructure for the solution. Security controls concerning the infrastructure include protecting the cloud service from natural disasters, having reliable backup systems and plans in place to backup data in the event of a hardware failure, and having policies and procedures in place regarding employee access to data and other internal security protocols.

ACTIVITY 4-3
Describing Data Integration

Scenario:

In this activity, you will review your knowledge on cloud data integration.

---

1. **Identify the challenges involved in data integration. (Choose all that apply.)**

   a) Speed of change

   b) Data distribution

   c) Data volumes

   d) Data privacy

---

2. **Identify the challenges involved in migrating data to the cloud.**

   a) Liability

   b) Data protection

   c) Data distribution

   d) Data interruption

TOPIC D
Security Risks and Mitigation

You identified the challenges associated with the data integration process. In addition to data integration, security is also a critical concern with cloud services. In this topic, you will identify the challenges associated with implementing cloud security.

The externalized aspect of cloud computing has rendered several challenges in implementing cloud security. To ensure data privacy and protection, it becomes inevitable for you to combat the challenges associated with implementing an effective cloud security system.

Security Risks

Security is the top concern for any organization that wants to implement cloud computing. There are several risks when you deploy a cloud service.

Security risks in cloud

Figure 4-4: The risk factors associated with cloud security.

Security Risk	Description
Lack of visibility	The data in the cloud is stored in multiple geographic locations and so the physical location of the data cannot be determined. This leads to a number of security and compliance issues, as the consumers are unaware of the physical storage location of their data.
Massive sharing	The concept of cloud computing revolves around the fact of sharing the computing resources between multiple organizations on a demand and usage basis. In the cloud, it is possible for misconfiguration, data compromise, and unauthorized access of information, because many users access data simultaneously.
Unwanted data disclosure	If the law demands data from a company that is being stored in the cloud, then the cloud provider is forced to disclose the data. This can be dangerous when the data is sensitive and may lead to customer dissatisfaction.

Security Risk	Description
Change in jurisdiction	If an organization with world-wide business stores its customer data in the cloud, it is forced to abide by the international compliance rules and restrictions. When different jurisdictions apply their own rules, the situation becomes complex because the risk of data being disclosed becomes much higher.

Cloud Service Models and Security Responsibility

Different models of cloud computing have various ways of exposing their underlying infrastructure to the user. This influences the control over infrastructure and the distribution of responsibilities for managing its security.

Cloud Type	Description
SaaS	In SaaS, the task of security management in cloud lies with the service provider. The providers adopt to numerous control measures to restrict the access of data in cloud such as: ● Identity management ● Access of data restricted to specific IP address ranges or physical locations ● And, application level configuration.
PaaS	In PaaS, the consumers or the clients are responsible to adopt to security measures such as: ● Managing the configuration and security for the middleware ● The Database ● And, application runtime environments.
IaaS	In IaaS, the responsibility of ensuring security lies with the client because the access is available to the operating system that supports virtual images, networking, and storage in cloud.

Implementing Security

The internal functioning of cloud services are not visible to users, which makes it hard to define, validate, and enforce security controls.

Challenge in Implementing Security	Description
Implementation of security controls	The cloud-based environment is prone to rapid changes and so, the time taken by organizations to deploy applications is very minimal. Enforcement of security controls in such a rapidly-changing environment is difficult as computing resources are spread over different physical locations in cloud.
Loss of control	As service providers outsource the infrastructure and applications to other providers to meet excessive demands of the customers there is a possibility for the loss of control in cloud which includes security of data.
Sharing of resources	The hardware or software resources of cloud are shared by many users. Such sharing introduces the possibility of security compromises in cloud such as unauthorized access of data.

Security Standards

To ensure data security and privacy protection, the cloud computing industry turns to several auditable standards. Each one comes with controls in a variety of categories that govern operation of a cloud provider's data center as well as the applications you move to the cloud.

Standard	Description
SAS (Statement on Auditing Standards) 70	In SAS 70, the cloud service providers can choose their own controls and the goals those controls intend to achieve. This standard includes controls to govern the physical security, application security, security policies and processes in the cloud.
PCI (Payment Card Industry)	PCI has stronger security norms when compared to SAS 70 as it adheres to more rigid compliance requirements. HIPAA (Health Insurance Portability and Accountability Act) compliance is a subset of the PCI compliance standards, which means that a cloud should be HIPAA compliant if it is PCI compliant.

CSA

The Cloud Security Alliance (CSA) is an organization that promotes the use of best practices for providing security assurance within cloud computing. It is governed by a coalition of industry practitioners, enterprises, associations and other key stakeholders.

Encryption

It is critical to protect the privacy of data and adhere to compliance standards when encrypting and managing encryption keys of data in transit to the cloud. Never store your encrypted data and the encryption keys on the same server. You cannot always trust the cloud provider for security. In addition to encrypting data stored on virtual systems, the companies should use encryption to properly authenticate employees who can access the data.

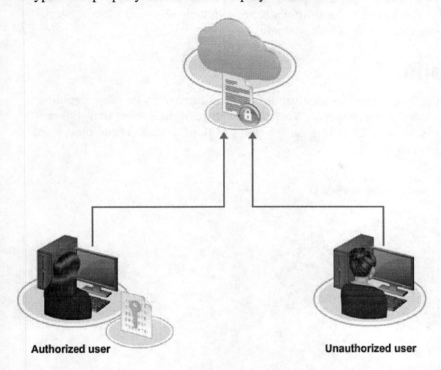

Authorized user **Unauthorized user**

Figure 4-5: Authorized users using the encryption key to access cloud services.

With data accumulating quickly, encrypting every bit of information is a tedious task. You need to identify the most valuable data and start the encryption project there. A best practice for companies dealing with information has to do with segregating who has what kind of access, deploying encryption in key areas, and then severely limiting who has access to the encryption components and data in its unencrypted form.

SSL Encryption

Secure Sockets Layer (SSL) encryption is a protocol for encrypting information over the Internet. The SSL creates a secure connection between two endpoints, allowing data to be sent securely. It uses two keys to encrypt the data being sent: a public key that is available to everyone and a private or secret key that only the recipient of the message would have access to.

Firewalls

A cloud firewall is a network firewall appliance specifically designed to work with cloud-based security solutions. It serves the same purposes as traditional firewalls, but it is different from a traditional firewall in three aspects: scalability, availability, and extensibility. Cloud firewalls are designed to scale as customer bandwidth increases, or at least any hardware upgrade has to be made transparent to customers. Cloud firewall providers offer extremely high availability through an infrastructure with fully redundant power and network services, as well as backup strategies in the event of a site failure. Cloud firewalls are available anywhere the network manager can provide a protected communications path.

Virtual Firewalls

A virtual firewall (VF) is software used to monitor and control the access of the computing resources in a virtual networking environment. Virtual firewalls can operate in two different modes to provide security services, depending on the point of deployment. These modes are the bridge-mode and hypervisor-mode.

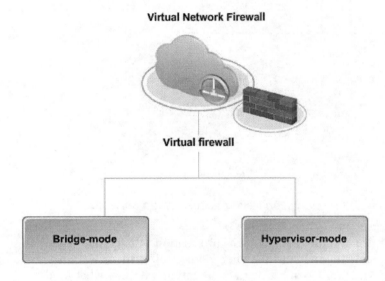

Figure 4-6: *A firewall devised to cater to the needs of virtual environments.*

Bridge-mode

A virtual firewall operating in bridge-mode examines the data packets for the source and destination addresses and verifies the validity of the data packet to be moved forward, dropped, rejected, or mirrored to some other device.

Hypervisor-mode

A hypervisor-mode is a virtual firewall which resides in the virtual machine monitor or hypervisor and captures the activities of the virtual machine in order to monitor data.

A hypervisor-mode virtual firewall is not a part of virtual network, and has no physical device. It resides in the virtual machine monitor or hypervisor and captures the activities of the virtual machine in order to monitor data.

Strategies to Ensure Security

It is difficult to find a "one size fits all" solution to ensure cloud security, following certain guidelines can help you implement and manage cloud security effectively.

- To implement and maintain security programs.
- To implement a data protection mechanism.
- To implement identity management system to access data in the cloud.
- To implement a vulnerability and intrusion management program.
- To implement compliance and audit management programs.

Security Programs

A security program ensures information security by identifying potential risks and threats to the target environment. In case of a security breach, the security program provides crucial information on the protection of cloud, responses to threats, and a line of accountability for management of events.

ACTIVITY 4-4
Describing Security Risks and Their Mitigation Measures

Scenario:

In this activity, you will review your knowledge on the security risks and their mitigation measures.

1. **Identify the challenges involved in implementing cloud security. (Choose all that apply.)**

   a) Scalability

   b) Security controls

   c) Sharing of resources

   d) Loss of control

2. **True or False? PCI is not a specific set of auditing standards; instead, cloud providers are responsible for choosing their own controls and the goals those controls intend to achieve.**

   ___ True

   ___ False

TOPIC E
Application Architecture and the Development Process

It is critical that you are aware of the underlying architecture and development process before you deploy an application over cloud or use a cloud application. In this topic, you will describe the application development process and the various application architectures available.

When you plan to develop an application that you want to deploy on cloud, you should have knowledge about the application development process, and the best practices involved in it such as the application architecture.

Application Development Process

A cloud application is a hybrid between traditional desktop applications and traditional web applications. It offers the same benefits that desktop and web applications do, without many drawbacks. The cloud application development process involves several stages.

1. Create a road map document in which you define the web application goals, purpose, and direction.
2. Define the audience by specifying their scope and level of access.
3. Identify and document application features.
4. Define technology specifications such as the platform, development environment, and application development framework.
5. Develop an application visual guide, including layout design and interface design.
6. Develop the web application by creating the application architecture, database structure, and develop application module.
7. Perform beta testing to produce the most secure and reliable application.

Application Lifecycle Management

Application Lifecycle Management (ALM) is a process of managing the life of an application in the cloud by developing, applying, and maintaining a set of governance standards. There are five important imperatives to consider when you are involved in ALM.

● Perform real-time planning. You need to ensure that the plans are fully integrated with project execution and always up to date so that you can track when your goals are accomplished.

● Implement lifecycle traceability. This helps you understand what everyone in the application management team is doing.

● Encourage collaboration. This can improve a team's ability to connect with each other, to respond to changes, and to improve project predictability.

● Implement development intelligence. This helps you understand whether your project is trending towards a successful outcome at any point in time.

● Implement continuous process improvement. This helps you manage changes by introducing marginal changes in the team to improve the process.

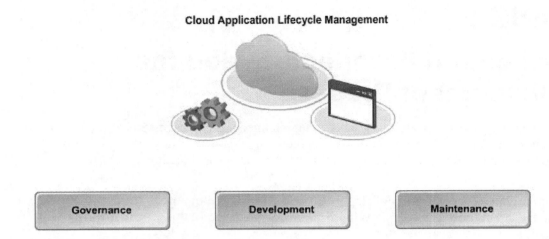

Figure 4-7: *The process of managing a cloud application.*

SOA

A *Service-Oriented Architecture (SOA)* is a structure used to instigate the communication among services. This communication can just involve the data transfer or two services coordinating with each other to perform an activity. Service interactions are defined using a description language and each interaction is self-contained and loosely coupled, so that each interaction is independent of the other.

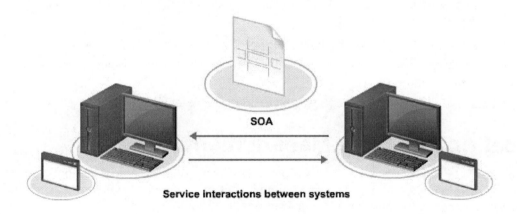

Figure 4-8: *The SOA enabling the interaction between two systems.*

Traditional Architecture

In a traditional architecture, calls for one or more web servers interact with the database via a middle-tier software framework. This architecture is designed to meet stable demand levels of the consumers to access the cloud resources, and it cannot tolerate huge variations in system load.

Multi-Tier Architecture

In a multi-tier application architecture, the processing of data and management of applications are implemented as separate logical processes. The application is broken up into multiple tiers or layers, which makes it easier to make a flexible and customizable application. A multi-tier application architecture allows the application developers to make changes to the entire application simply by modifying a specific tier in the application. The division of an application into tiers enables the developers to modify any part of that application without having to change the other parts. This proves to be advantageous to the developers as they specialize in designing specific tier or tiers of an application. A common multi-tier architecture is a three-tier architecture. The components in each tier perform a specific type of processing – there's a user services tier, a business services tier, and a data services tier.

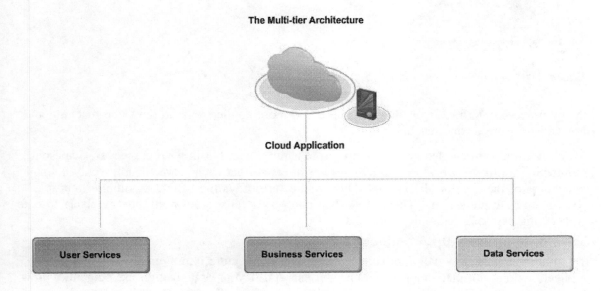

Figure 4-9: *The division of the cloud application into three layers.*

Scale-Up and Scale-Out Architecture

When you need more power, you get a bigger, more powerful server. This is referred to as *scale-up architecture* and has become the de facto standard for gaining more power in data centers. The ability to scale to larger numbers of processors within a single server continues to grow, and as a result, engineers create immensely powerful servers, containing the improved data systems all within a new, more powerful package. However, disaster recovery becomes a challenge with these systems.

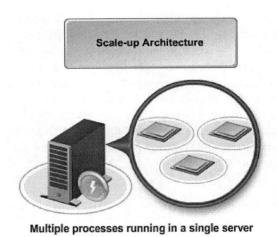

Multiple processes running in a single server

Figure 4-10: *A single server handling multiple processes.*

As the processors grow larger, they run more and more applications on the same machine and thus add pressure to one machine.

Scale-out architectures also provide more processing power, but in a different way. Scale-out architectures split the workload over multiple servers so that each server handles only a small percentage of the load of all systems. This architecture offers the benefit of running multiple systems on multiple servers. Therefore, when one server fails, other nodes are available to take over, taking care of availability concerns.

Scale-out vs. Scale-up Architecture

If you are using many small applications, scale-out architecture is preferable. You can put the applications on multiple, smaller, and cheaper servers. If your organization uses gigantic, powerhouse applications, then a scale-up architecture is a good choice because it is more cost-effective compared to having a larger set of machines.

Synchronous Application Architecture

In synchronous applications, such as websites, end-user interaction is the primary concern. A large number of users try to access the same application simultaneously, which may overload the system's capacity to meet the demands and result in poor performance. A synchronous application architecture provides enough web servers to handle high volumes of traffic and enough middleware to manage the high demand simultaneously. If demand exceeds the web server layer, the middleware gets overloaded. The middle layer of a synchronous application architecture must be designed to scale to meet increased demands as well. In addition, the architecture provides a data tier that scales, which enables you to avoid exceeding a database.

Asynchronous Application Architecture

Asynchronous applications are focused on information processing rather than end-user interaction, and occasionally handle large loads of data, which requires a different architecture model. An asynchronous application architecture uses a separate functionality to process components that can be linked by a queue mechanism. The queue mechanism is ideal for load balancing. The output of one component is made available to the next component in the chain. If that component is unable to take on the load from the previous component, the work item is pushed into a queue, where it waits for the next available component to read the data and perform the required task.

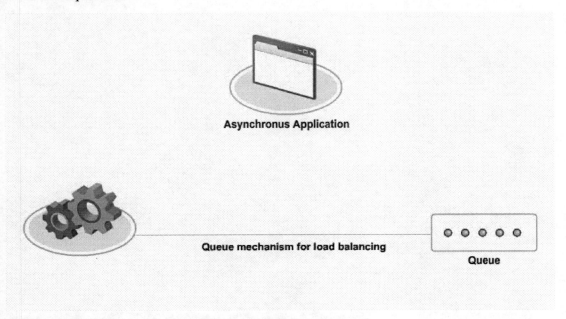

Asynchronus Application

Queue mechanism for load balancing

Queue

Figure 4-11: Jobs to be processed are assigned in a queue.

Open Security Architecture

The *Open Security Architecture (OSA)* is an architecture framework that can be used during the design and integration of security and controls for IT solutions. Applying OSA gives you a fast start in your work, improves the quality of the solution you deploy, and reduces overall effort. An open approach means that the patterns and catalogs will benefit the whole community of IT security administrators and can be more quickly improved and refined by the common experience of participants.

Cloud Emulators

An *emulator* is a hardware or software module or both that duplicates the functions of one computer system in another computer system, so that the latter resembles the former. In cloud computing, emulators are software often used for smooth migration from one cloud to another without having to redevelop API based tools. A compute emulator can simulate the desired environment on your local computer, so that you can run and test your new application on your local computer before you deploy it.

ACTIVITY 4-5

Describing Application Architecture and Development Process

Scenario:

In this activity, you will review your knowledge on application architecture and development process.

---

1. **True or False? The traditional architecture is designed to balance heavy work load in the cloud.**

   __ True

   __ False

---

2. **Identify the architecture that splits the workload over multiple servers to improve processing power.**

   a) Traditional application

   b) Scale-up

   c) Scale-out

   d) Multi-tier application

Lesson 4 Follow-up

You identified the technical challenges involved and the mitigation measures in cloud computing. This knowledge enables you to prepare yourself for cloud migration.

1. **What are the critical challenges of cloud storage? Why?**

2. **Do you think encrypting data in the cloud helps improve security? How?**

5 | Steps to Successful Adoption of Cloud Services

Lesson Time: 1 hour(s), 45 minutes

Lesson Objectives:

In this lesson, you will identify the steps to successfully adopt cloud services.

You will:

● Identify the steps to adopt cloud services.

● Identify the organization's readiness for cloud services adoption.

● Describe the roles and capabilities of a cloud vendor.

● Understand the approaches for migrating applications to the cloud.

Introduction

You are now aware of the various services offered by cloud computing. You may want to deploy one or more of these services in your organization. In this lesson, you will learn how to successfully adopt cloud services.

Organizations have to develop and execute a plan to meet the business and technical needs of an organization. Even after making significant investments in infrastructure and technologies such as SOA, it is important to identify critical factors to adopt cloud computing so that the new cloud service can be positioned on a previously available on-premise data center.

TOPIC A
Steps to Adopting Cloud Services

The first action you should take when considering implementing cloud computing is to identify what is involved in the adoption process. In this topic, you will identify the steps to adopt cloud services.

Before you perform a procedure, wouldn't you want to know the procedure step by step? In a similar way, to deploy a cloud service, you need to identify the steps to successfully transition to cloud computing.

Cloud Adoption Evaluation Factors

IT organizations should evaluate the need to choose a specific cloud deployment model based on the type of services rendered. Determining the movement of IT operations to cloud based operations relies on these factors:

- The different types of services offered by cloud providers, and adherence to a specific service based on their requirements.

- The service management capabilities of the chosen service model, such as the cost of operations, metering etc.

- The challenge areas in adopting a specific cloud service model, such as the integration pattern, the standards adopted for ensuring data security, and integrity.

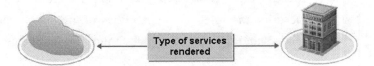

Figure 5-1: The factor that evaluates the adoption of cloud services.

Critical Success Factors

The demands on business IT infrastructure have increased dramatically and companies have been rapidly adopting cloud services. Yet, not all cloud adoptions are successful. There are certain critical success factors that will help you carry out the cloud adoption process successfully.

- Choose an appropriate service model based on enterprise needs.

- Identify an appropriate deployment model such as a public, private, or hybrid cloud.

- Conduct a security audit of the present on-premises system and find whether the lack of security of a cloud deployment outweighs the required advantages.

- Choose an appropriate cloud vendor with a long-standing position in the market and a strong background.

- Create an SLA that outlines all your requirements, as well as the cloud vendors, with proper and adequate coverage of critical needs.

- Calculate the economic benefits from cloud services.

- Take appropriate change management measures for the changes that cloud computing may bring.

• Quantify the advantages and disadvantages of cloud computing by taking the size of the company into consideration.

The Cloud Adoption Process

A successful cloud computing adoption must focus on the areas of trust, security, legal compliance, and organizational issues. The road map for successful cloud adoption involves five phases: analysis, planning, adoption, migration, and management.

1. In the analysis phase, the existing systems, applications, and business processes are analyzed by the analysts in association with the users. Also, the impact of migrating to the cloud is analyzed, and the potential cloud vendor is identified.

2. In the planning phase, the platforms for deployment, the cloud infrastructure, finance plan, security, legal compliance plan, and the roll-out plan for the adoption project are chosen by the management. The objectives and the direction for adopting cloud computing is set in this phase.

3. In the adoption phase, application integration with cloud platforms and infrastructure, outsourcing strategies, SLAs, security policies, and legal compliance management are carried out by the analysts and the project team as well.

4. In the migration phase, the application and data migration are carried out by the management as per the specifications given in the migration plan that was developed during the planning phase. The availability of user support during the migration process is ensured in this phase.

5. In the management phase, project sign off and review of the entire project are carried out. The best practices and the lessons learned are documented. Continuous technical support for the system and the users is ensured by the management team.

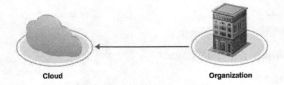

Figure 5-2: *An organization adopting cloud computing.*

Cloud Selection Criteria

An important part of adopting cloud computing is choosing the service provider best-suited to your specific needs. The overall reliability of your cloud-based service depends on the quality of the cloud service provider. The four most important criteria that enable you to evaluate a cloud service provider are redundancy, service level agreements, historical performance, and service optimization.

Criteria	Description
Service level agreements	The Service Level Agreement (SLA) that stipulates the guaranteed percentage of service uptime should be investigated. This provides a measurement on the availability that can be expected from the cloud service.
Historical performance	A record of the service uptime and reliable IT solutions should be demonstrated by the cloud service provider. Historical performance of a service provider is a good indicator of their future performance.
Redundancy	The redundancy in power, Internet, heating, ventilation, and air conditioning (HVAC) systems in the data center of the service provider should be investigated.
Monitoring and performance optimization	The confirmation on optimal level of service that can be provided by the cloud provider should be determined.

Vendor Selection Process

When planning to implement cloud computing for the first time, many organizations wonder how to choose the right vendor. The selection process is not much different from the process that you would follow in making any technology purchase decision. There are three phases involved in the vendor selection process.

1. Analyze your organization.

   ● Analyze your current IT infrastructure.

   ● Determine your goals and challenges.

   ● Identify the traffic spikes.

2. Draw an outline with the critical criteria that determines your desired cloud vendor.

   ● Determine the scalability required.

   ● Determine the level of security required.

   ● Identify the desirable server configuration.

3. Compare cloud vendors based on the selected criteria.

   ● Identify their ability to automatically set up additional servers.

   ● Determine your access to low-level resources.

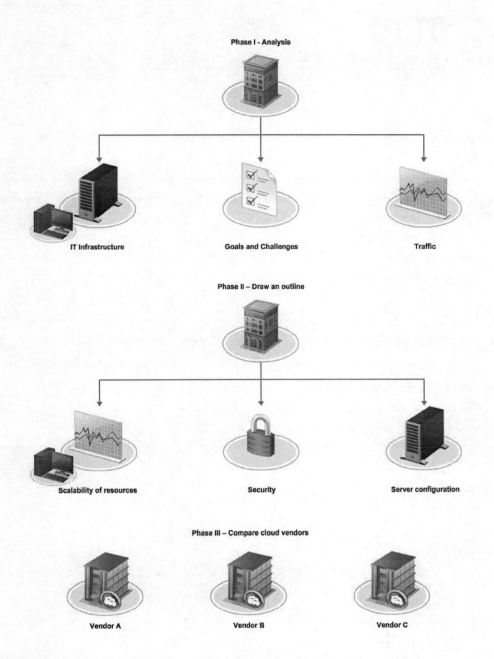

Upgrade and Maintenance Schedules

Cloud vendors have to upgrade their systems in regular intervals in order to install the enhanced security patches and features. Users that access applications that are running in the cloud will need to be aware when such patches are happening. Accordingly, a plan should be in place so that they are not adversely affected. Vendors often give an option to decide when the upgrade will take place and specify a fixed final deadline when it will happen anyway. So, the application developers should carry out testing well in advance to ensure service continuity.

ACTIVITY 5-1
Identifying the Steps to Adopt Cloud Services

Scenario:
In this activity, you will review your knowledge of the steps to adopt cloud services.

1. **Identify the feature that helps you determine the level of service provided by the cloud vendor.**

   a) Historical performance

   b) Redundancy

   c) Monitoring

   d) SLA

2. **What is the first step involved in the vendor selection process?**

   a) Drawing an outline with the critical criteria that determines the desired cloud vendor.

   b) Analyzing the organization.

   c) Comparing cloud vendors based on the selected criteria.

   d) Finalizing the cloud vendor.

TOPIC B

Organizational Capability to Adopt Cloud Services

You identified the steps for adopting cloud services. Your organizational capabilities have a great influence in the cloud adoption process. In this topic, you will identify the organizational capabilities needed to adopt cloud services.

When you try to adopt something new, wouldn't you want to know your current abilities so that you can identify the gap between what you have and what you need? Similarly, identifying your present organizational capabilities helps you to determine whether you are ready to adopt cloud services efficiently.

Cloud Readiness

A cloud migration plan involves five steps:

1. The current environment should be optimized by providing an internal set of cloud services, and also enabling the adoption of external services.

2. Cloud service opportunities should be identified based on business needs, and the organization's ability to adopt those services.

3. Communication with other business units should be done about cloud services, the road map, and the process for incorporating them into the architecture.

4. Pilot projects should be undertaken with various services to identify areas that might create issues.

5. A cross-functional team should be designated to continuously monitor the new services, providers, and standards that meet organization's needs, and determine if it affects the road map.

Infrastructure Management

Cloud infrastructure management involves managing and providing support for clients' cloud infrastructure, and also providing specific cloud-based IT operations. Managing the business email on cloud infrastructure, building and maintaining a data center at a minimal cost, providing virtual machines on demand, and providing automated, secure and cost efficient methods for backup are some of the infrastructure management operations.

Service Management

Cloud service management involves techniques and tools for managing services across environments, both physical and virtual. Service management is comprised of various disciplines, including asset management, capacity planning, configuration management, workload management, network management, service desk, problem-solving and analysis, and update management. An integration of core service management capabilities and well-defined interfaces make up a well-designed cloud service portfolio.

Risk Management

When organizations think of migrating to cloud services, they face three kinds of risks: business, technical, and legal. Business risks include vendor lock in, data management, and termination of cloud service. The technical risks include exhaustion of resources and hacking of data. Legal risks include unwanted data disclosure and licensing issues.

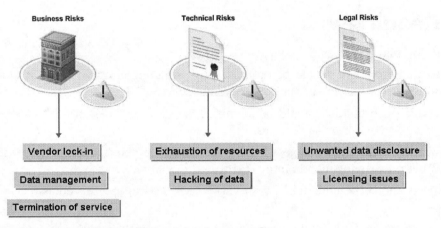

Figure 5-3: *The potential risks involved in cloud.*

Experts suggest several risk management measures to face critical risks associated with cloud computing.

Risk Management Technique	Description
Performance Measurement	Measuring cloud performance enables you to ensure that IT performance is good enough to support business, customers get appropriate responses to requests, data is safe from unauthorized access, and management gets the right information when needed and can recover from anticipated outages without hindering customer loyalty.
Record documentation	Many organizations record IT services and resources using a service catalog. This has information on the person in charge of the service, the authority that can change the service, critical applications related to the service, relationship among services, and all agreements between the cloud provider and the organization.

Risk Management Technique	Description
Resource tracking	To ensure efficient performance, you need to keep track of the changes that cloud resources undergo. For instance, many cloud providers use virtualization extensively to improve efficiency. But, multiple usage of hardware assets increases the difficulty of tracking changes to these resources.
Security management	You are likely to encounter security risks, threats, and breaches in several forms and from several places. Therefore, you need to take a comprehensive approach to secure your data and applications. You can ensure security in a cloud environment in three ways: identity management, detection and forensics, and data encryption.

Financial Management

Scaling up IT operations and services in preparation for cloud computing may result in increased expenditures for the organization. New hardware and software licenses may need to be purchased to set up a data center. When cloud services are adopted, it makes the most financial sense to only pay for the resources that will be used. This reduces the capital expenditure, thereby enabling maximum potential returns.

A crucial factor in financial management is the design and development of a detailed plan. The plan should include determining which type of cloud can minimize cost planning, performing a risk analysis of the assets that are involved, developing contingency cost allocation plans, and assessing the business requirements of the organization.

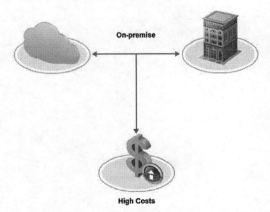

Figure 5-4: The on-premise model denoting the high capital expenditure.

Vendor Management

Organizations hoping to move their operations to a cloud environment must choose a suitable vendor to ensure consistent usage of the cloud services. You can adopt several measures to manage vendors.

- Modify your business and functional processes to take advantage of moving the operations to cloud.

- Focus on analyzing the requirements and vendor management.

- Conduct third party audits to ensure the security of their data, monitor cloud services and vendors.

- Monitor the integrated cloud services in a federated cloud environment, just in case there is a need to hold the vendors responsible for breach of trust.

ACTIVITY 5-2

Identifying the Organizational Capability to Adopt Cloud Services

Scenario:

In this activity, you will review your knowledge on identifying the organizational capability to adopt cloud services.

1. **Identify the activities that help you determine cloud readiness. (Choose all that apply.)**

   a) Optimize the current environment by providing an internal set of cloud services and enabling the incorporation of external services.

   b) Draft the Service Level Agreement (SLA).

   c) Designate a cross-functional team to monitor cloud services.

   d) Undertake pilot projects with various services.

2. **What are the tasks involved in drafting a plan for cloud migration? (Choose all that apply.)**

   a) Run "what-if" analysis to make build vs. buy cloud computing decisions such as on-premise private cloud, hosted private cloud, and public cloud.

   b) Determine cost and value trade-offs of your cloud computing architectures.

   c) Design and manage cloud performance KPIs such as unit rate reduction goals and return on assets (ROA).

   d) Analyze the organization.

TOPIC C
Cloud Vendor Roles and Capabilities

You identified the organizational capabilities needed to adopt cloud services. Next, you need to understand the capabilities of your cloud service provider to be able to analyze the quality of service. In this topic, you will describe the roles and capabilities of a cloud vendor.

Just as the quality of a product is directly related to the quality of the seller, the quality of a cloud service is very much dependent on the capabilities of a cloud vendor.

Cloud Client Business Requirements

The key characteristic feature of cloud computing is the ability to share the resource pool across multiple organizations, also known as multi-tenancy. A cloud client would want to make utmost use of these shared resources to satisfy their business needs.

Client Business Requirement	Description
An open, standard–based server model	Consumers may require an environment to use complex applications (SaaS) in the cloud. Some cloud service providers maintain a framework based on proprietary languages, which may not be suitable for many consumers. It is essential for providers to maintain an open, Java-based model to support SaaS applications.
End-user personalization	Consumers might expect to have the privilege to control the application user interface. Additionally, they might want to customize the basic look and feel of their application by creating logos and deciding the color patterns for the applications etc. Providers should be able to deliver a framework whereby the consumers are able to customize their application templates.
Internationalization and accessibility	Any application development should be designed to support internationalization and accessibility requisites.
Denial of access by unauthorized users	Consumers expect that data stored in the cloud is secure and safe from unauthorized access. Service providers should build a security mechanism to integrate the server-side and consumer-side data security such that unauthorized use of data can be eradicated.

Types of Services Offered by Cloud Vendors

Several cloud services are available in the market, but only a few services are widely adopted by organizations.

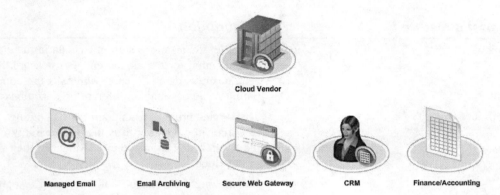

Figure 5-5: *Different services provided by the cloud vendor.*

Cloud service	Description
Email Management	Service providers provide cloud services that work well at your physical business site and that can also be customized to be applied on your mobile devices such as iPhones, Blackberries and other smartphones.
Secure Web Gateway	The web gateway is a security solution which monitors the operations of the cloud network and restricts unauthorized users from accessing the data.
Finance/Accounting	Cloud vendors hold the responsibility of handling the complete accounting procedure involved in the entire transaction with the client to use the cloud services such as hosting the software applications, process the data, integrate it with taxes and payroll processing, expenses and other business needs.
Email Archiving	With storage and retrieval of data being the key components of cloud, it is possible to store an unlimited amount of email, to provide your business with a clear audit trail.
Customer Relationship Management (CRM)	The cloud vendors typically aim at building a set of functionalities to improve the interactions with clients, in order to adopt cost effective measures and effectively handle business transactions. Examples of cloud vendors handling CRM are: Salesforce.com and Dynamics.

Key Characteristics of a Cloud Vendor

While each cloud computing vendor will operate with a slightly different business plan, all reputable vendors share key characteristics.

Characteristic feature	Description
Multi-tenancy	Multiple organizations store their data in the cloud. It is essential for the cloud vendors to ensure that each business data is secure, while sharing computing resources among different organizations.
Self-service	The service providers maintain the computing resources in cloud, and it is the responsibility of the organization to maintain and manage their data in the cloud.
Scalability	Maximizing the utilization of computing resources is the key feature of cloud. Therefore, it is the responsibility of the cloud vendor to provide services irrespective of the number of users and the amount of data an organization holds.
Redundant data storage	Cloud vendors store multiple copies of customer data in different physical sites, to enable cloud computing be suitable for businesses that need high availability.
Affordability	Since the cloud operations are based on demand and usage basis, it is essential for the users to enter into an agreement with the vendor which defines the cost of acquiring the services, and the term of usage which is always flexible to cater to the needs of the business.

Criteria for Selecting a Vendor

The cloud market is flooded with thousands of products and services. However, not all vendors can deliver the real benefits of cloud. To select a suitable vendor, you need to analyze certain critical criteria.

● Facilitate workshops to identify detailed business, applications, and platform and infrastructure requirements.

● Identify potential solutions: SaaS, PaaS, IaaS, and other managed services vendors.

● Develop RFP evaluation criteria, scoring and vetting process.

● Identify interoperability, lock-in, and compatibility issues and determine workarounds as applicable.

● Facilitate vendor negotiations and selection processes.

Carry out a hands-on product and technology validation and evaluation against the above criteria and perform proof-of-concepts to see how a vendor's offering really works and how it fits into the requirements of your business. Through this process, you can become familiar with constraints, issues and benefits of the technology.

Criterion	Description
Experience	Cloud computing is an emerging technology and many players are entering the market lately. You need to investigate how long they've been providing the service.
Ability to meet business needs	Determine to what extent the vendor meets your detailed requirements.
Ease of Setup and Maintenance	Determine the time the vendor will take to get the initial environment set up and how they will maintain it thereafter.
Portability	Determine whether they use tools that are easily portable in case you need to move to another vendor; for example, because of a change in the organization's requirements.
Ease of Maintenance	Investigate whether the vendor is flexible enough to add services or change the functionality.
Ease of Integration	The vendor should be able to integrate your data easily on to the cloud and provide you the data when you require it.
Security	Many applications are critical and have sensitive data. Make sure it is protected.
Legal/Compliance	For sensitive data, ensure that the provider meets legal and regulatory requirements such as SAS 70 or HIPAA compliance.

Vendor Liability

The cloud vendor has extensive liabilities due to the nature and requirements of a shared infrastructure.

Liability	Description
Cost of operations	The providers do not include all the charges incurred to use cloud services in their fee schedules. Costs pertaining to add-on services such as security, monitoring, data transfer and back-up may not be included in the fee structure. Providers should make sure that the cost for all services rendered by them is mentioned in the agreement.
Planned maintenance	It is essential for providers to deliver uninterrupted and secured services to consumers. Providers should clearly define their maintenance plan schedules in the SLA so that consumers can plan their activities accordingly.
Data Security	Providers are completely liable for the security of data held in the cloud. Terms and conditions should be defined clearly in the SLA for unauthorized access of data, corruption, deletion or destruction of data. In the event of a security breach, providers are held liable for compensation.

Data Integrity

The data on the cloud is location independent and it can be accessed by any number of users. Since critical and non-critical data of multiple organizations are stored in the cloud, it is harder to maintain data integrity and privacy.

There are several ways in which you can minimize the threats to data integrity:

- Maintaining identity management systems to restrict the unauthorized access to data and applications.
- Implementing error detection and correction software for data in transit.
- Adopting data backup plans that will occur at regular time intervals.
- Designing and utilizing suitable user interfaces that prevent users from possibly entering invalid data.

ACTIVITY 5-3
Describing Roles and Capabilities of a Cloud Vendor

Scenario:
In this activity, you will review your knowledge of the roles and capabilities of a cloud vendor.

1. **Identify ways to minimize threats to data integrity. (Choose all that apply.)**

   a) Determine how well the vendor meets your detailed requirements.

   b) Back up data regularly.

   c) Control access to data using security mechanisms.

   d) Design user interfaces that prevent the input of invalid data.

2. **True or False? The externalized aspect of outsourcing makes it harder to maintain data integrity and privacy.**

   ___ True

   ___ False

TOPIC D
Migrating Applications to the Cloud

You described the roles and capabilities of a cloud vendor. The final step in the cloud adoption process is to identify the right approach for migrating your applications on to the cloud. In this topic, you will describe the various approaches for migrating applications to the cloud.

To be able to identify the most suitable migration method for your business and IT needs, you need to understand the various methods available.

Key Aspects for Migration

Certain key aspects accelerate the migration of applications to the cloud environment. An organization has to consider many key factors such as criticality, elasticity, governance, and technology when migrating to cloud services. It is essential to understand the business value that cloud services would offer to its client and how an organization or a cloud provider can adapt to suit the requirements in terms of workload, storage, and utilization. It is also essential to understand whether cloud providers offer security, service management, risk management, and compliance checks for cloud services and whether an appropriate technology, architecture, and infrastructure are in place to offer better quality of cloud services.

Shared Services

The availability of shared resources in the cloud infrastructure is an important key factor for the success of cloud computing. The hardware, applications, servers, network, and storage available in the cloud environment can be accessed and shared by any tenant as a metered service via the Internet. Cloud consumers can access these shared resources from a centralized location and benefit from the maximum utilization of them.

Multi-tenancy

Definition:

The sharing of cloud services or cloud resources among multiple users (or tenants) either within or outside an enterprise is referred to as multi-tenancy. A tenant can be any application or resource who needs a secure virtual environment for their services. There are various layers in a cloud architecture and multi-tenancy varies from the hardware layer to a user-interface layer depending on the degree of cloud services offered by the cloud provider, and varies according to the design of the core application.

Example:

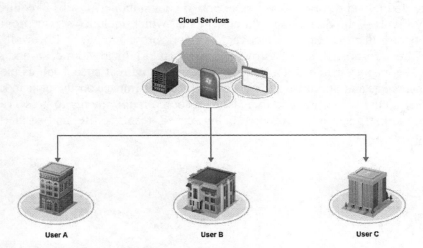

Figure 5-6: Multiple tenants using shared resources in the cloud infrastructure.

Patterns of Cloud Migration

The cloud infrastructure can be hosted in four different patterns, such as:

- Application re-hosting: Cloud consumers can virtually benefit using this pattern of cloud infrastructure because they can migrate to the cloud services with their current architecture mirrored to the cloud deployment model. It creates multiple instances of the application to improve scalability resulting in the reduction of operational expenditure (OpEX). This pattern helps to prevent failovers without incurring additional capital expenditure (CapEx).

- Service facade: This pattern works together with the application re-hosting pattern to provide the REST or SOAP service interface allowing program access to re-hosted applications. The pattern is not specific to application migration, but requires a wrapper around the native API of the existing application where the required schema is provided and protocol conversion takes place to provide the service interface. It decodes the application for cloud consumers, provides platform independent interoperability, and is applicable to re-hosting applications.

- Re-host and optimize: In this pattern, the application is managed by writing to a queue and reading from a cache. The queue front ends the application and helps to smooth out peaks in transactions while the cache takes the load off the application for simple reads.

- Re-architect: In this pattern, to address the business requirements and meet the demands of the agile architecture of software services, applications are restructured into a series of independent services with automation units that encapsulate their own data. Each unit is known as an integrity unit and can be deployed independently with its SLAs optimized to suit its unique profile.

Migration and Implementation Costs

It is essential to define and develop a workable cost model suitable for all IT requirements. The complexity involves the derivation of a cost model, which includes server provision, backups, various software licenses, disaster recovery, network provisioning, and firewall configuration. Direct costs such as infrastructure cost, network bandwidth cost, and software license cost can be easily evaluated and managed, whereas indirect costs such as electricity cost, maintenance cost, and administration cost have a direct impact on the cost model. Other factors that affect a cost model include forecast of resource requirements to be served in the upcoming time, market price of the resource being served, resource life, and service requirements for resources.

ACTIVITY 5-4
Migrating Applications to the Cloud

Scenario:

In this activity, you will review your knowledge on migrating applications to the cloud.

1. **Identify the cloud migration pattern that is most appropriate for the separation of application logic and database components in the current application.**

   a) Service facade pattern

   b) Re-host and optimize

   c) Application re-hosting

   d) Re-architect

2. **Identify the degree of multi-tenancy that allows the database schema to be shared and supports customization of the business logic and user-interface layers.**

   a) Lowest

   b) Middle

   c) Highest

Lesson 5 Follow-up

In this lesson, you identified the steps to successfully adopt cloud services. This knowledge will help you to plan and execute your migration process effectively.

1. **Which do you think is the most critical step in adopting cloud services?**

2. **What is the most critical characteristic of a good vendor? Why?**

6 | ITIL and Cloud Computing

Lesson Time: 3 hour(s), 15 minutes

Lesson Objectives:

In this lesson, you will identify the basic concepts of ITIL and describe how the ITIL framework is useful in the implementation of cloud computing in an organization.

You will:

- Identify and analyze the basic concepts of ITIL and how the service management framework of ITIL is useful for Cloud implementation.

- Briefly explain the various stages involved in the Service Strategy phase of the ITIL Lifecycle and how to transform service management into a strategic asset.

- Identify the various concepts of the Service Design phase of the ITIL Lifecycle.

- Briefly explain the various stages involved in the Service Transition phase and what value Service Transition provides to the business.

- Briefly explain the various concepts of the Service Operation phase of the ITIL Lifecycle and how the cloud services are delivered with acceptable level of service.

- Briefly explain the various concepts of the Continual Service Improvement (CSI) phase of the ITIL lifecycle and identify ways to create and maintain values over time.

Introduction

Organizations today are facing many technical challenges like scalability, availability, agility, shorter time to market, and increasing complexity. To manage applications on-premise and the cloud, organizations today follow ITIL to manage their data centers both in the traditional environment and the new environment. In this lesson, you will identify the basic concepts of ITIL and describe how ITIL can be applied to cloud operations in either on-premise data center or cloud environment.

Enterprises today need a hybrid management environment which will include both the on-premise and new cloud environment. The challenge is to adapt to the changes that will originate with the association of cloud as well as have an integrated mechanism to handle both the data center and cloud services.

TOPIC A
Overview of ITIL

You want to align your organization's IT practices with the cloud service, and ensure that it delivers an optimal value to all other business units of the organization. Before you start, you need to familiarize yourself with the fundamental concepts of ITIL, and the various phases of the Service Lifecycle that can be adopted and molded to fit in an organization. In this topic, you will describe the basic concepts of ITIL and outline the best practices that will apply to your organization.

In order to reach the comfort level where ITIL ideas can be applied, you will need a solid foundation in understanding the basic concepts of ITIL, where ITIL came from, what it does, and how it uniquely categorizes information in the IT service industry. Identifying and familiarizing yourself with the various phases of Service Lifecycle will help you to align the IT infrastructure of the organization with the cloud services.

Service Management

Definition:

Service Management is a set of specialized organizational capabilities for providing value to customers in the form of services. In service management, cloud services are aligned to problems and are tracked in a way that clearly demonstrates the value of the cloud service to internal or external customers.

Example: Managing Services at InfiniTrade Financial

Jeff is a Desktop Support Technician in the Financial industry. The particular IT service he performs daily involves maintaining and troubleshooting the desktop computers used at large global headquarters. When a problem occurs with a desktop computer in the building, the user reports the issue through an online tracking database that logs the necessary information and assigns it a ticket number. This ticket number is routed through a program that identifies which technician has both the expertise and the available time to assist with the issue. The online tracking tool is constantly being reviewed to see how effective it is, both in terms of the speed of response and the accuracy of the employee assignment.

Both the tool itself and the review of the tool are examples of service management; Jeff merely being able to provide desktop support alone is not sufficient. The real value from the customer's perspective is realized when Jeff provides an efficient and effective solution to the business problems related to failures on the desktops.

ITSM

IT Service Management (ITSM) is an aspect of Service Management that focuses on the technology involved in delivering a service. ITSM considers the assets, technical processes, and staff needed to operate the service. Effective service management allows a service provider to not only support the core business, but also deliver service value by facilitating the desired outcome that customers want to achieve.

Figure 6-1: *Implementation of ITSM in an organization.*

Business Service Management (BSM)

On the other end of the spectrum is the *Business Service Management (BSM)*, which is an approach to Service Management that considers the supported business processes and the added business value. It helps to ensure that the IT service provider is properly aligning its investments with the business objectives.

ITIL

The *IT Infrastructure Library (ITIL)*, a cohesive series of best standards of ITSM, is used to design an IT framework of an organization. It is widely accepted as a popular standard, both in public and private sectors globally, and is useful for providing guidance to any type of business or organization with an IT infrastructure. ITIL, being a leading best practice for service management, supports organizations in reducing risks and gaining maximum benefits from cloud computing.

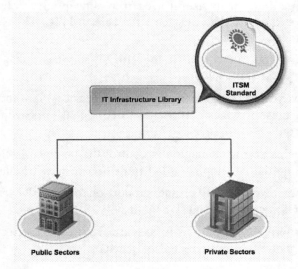

Figure 6-2: *The ITIL framework.*

History of ITIL

ITIL began in England in the late 1980s as a project by the Central Computer and Telecommunications Agency (CCTA). This agency produced a series of books devoted to the systematic delivery of quality IT services in the UK and the Netherlands, but the library quickly became global. Over time, this library has grown and has been modified with the addition of best practices from around the IT service industry. It has become a successful and popular framework.

ITIL Updates

An update version of ITIL was released on 29 July 2011 to meet the industry requirements. The updates include some improvements and suggested changes to the ITIL framework. Around 55 new terms have been included to the ITIL glossary and some 33 terms have been deleted. The current information for ITIL can be obtained from **www. itil-officialsite.com**.

Benefits of ITIL

Some of the key benefits of ITIL include:

- Improved IT services, resulting in the increased business productivity, efficiency, and effectiveness.

- Improved resource management and service usage, resulting in financial savings, less rework, and lost time.

- Improved user and customer satisfaction through a more professional approach to service delivery.

- Improved delivery of third party service.

- Improved time to market for new products and services.

- Improved decision making and optimized risk.

The Service Lifecycle

Every IT service has a time line for its useful life, from conception to obsolescence. These stages of development are known as the Service Lifecycle in ITIL. The Service Lifecycle consists of five phases:

- Service Strategy helps you to create a strategy for all services that will provide quality services to customers and stakeholders.

- Service Design helps you to design and deploy new services and applications, and ensure that the objective of these services contributes to continual improvement of the quality of services throughout the entire lifecycle.

- Service Transition helps you to manage and control the changes in the live operational environment, including the development and transition of new or changed IT services.

- Service Operation helps you to deliver and support operational IT services to achieve business and deliver forecasted business benefits.

- Continual Service Improvement helps you to learn from experience and adopting an approach to ensure continual improvement of services.

Each phase has its own core book in ITIL v3, and covers a variety of crucial elements in service management. While there are phase-specific events, some broader ideas are generated regardless of the Lifecycle phase:

- What is expected during a given phase?

- How the phase can be better managed and measured?

- Who participates in each phase and in what capacity?

- and, how to learn from and improve the service at every stage?

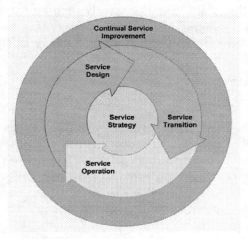

Figure 6-3: *The Service Lifecycle.*

Service Strategy

Definition:

Service Strategy lies at the center of the IT Service Lifecycle and concerns the overall strategic planning of the IT service. Service strategy encompasses portfolio, demand, and financial management, and forms a foundation stone for cloud computing. During the service strategy phase, you need to clearly define what services an organization needs, who needs them, and what resources are required to create and run the services. This includes determining the financial value of services offered and addresses any definition of value that the service is intended to provide to the customer throughout a service's entire lifecycle.

In addition to monitoring the demands, service strategy also helps influence off-peak prices to mitigate spikes in demand. For successful cloud computing, it involves careful planning of which service strategy to adopt, such as to improve a current service or to implement a new service.

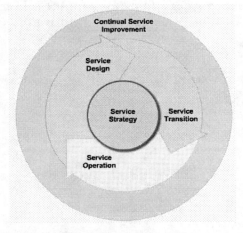

Figure 6-4: *The Service Strategy phase within the Service Lifecycle.*

Example: Service Strategy in a Restructuring Effort

Vicki is an analyst for Hexa Web Hosting Services, which has just announced a large restructuring effort to revamp its hosting plans. She is currently figuring out what the wage costs would be if the UNIX hosting packages become two, three, or four times as popular. Determining and managing labor costs are part of the Service Strategy Lifecycle phase.

Service Design

Definition:

Service Design is a phase in the lifecycle of an IT service that focuses on the design and development of services, service management processes, and any other related processes. The need for Service Design typically comes from a customer, internal or external, who has requested new or changed services. Service Design helps you to design IT services along with the governing IT practices, processes, and policies to facilitate the transition of services into the live operational environment, ensuring quality service delivery, customer satisfaction, and cost-effective service provision.

When employing external cloud services, it is essential to calculate availability requirements for all services and applications that will utilize cloud. Measurement tools should be installed to ensure that availability levels are maintained within the acceptable service level usage, avoiding unplanned cloud usage and additional charges.

Other service design functions include:

- Capacity management ensures that capacity levels meet the planned growth expectations. If the capacity exceeds the level, the cloud supplier will be charged extra. It is essential that exact service continuity requirements for external cloud services are verified and updated frequently.

- Protection of sensitive and confidential information from malware attacks in the external cloud and applications. It is critical to place safeguards to prevent security breaches. Contractual agreements should be verified so that external cloud suppliers are obliged to meet the agreed level of service.

- Service Catalog management ensures that there is a service catalog for each cloud provider and that all catalogs integrate with in-house services for the delivery of quality service.

- Service Level Management provides a framework for the delivery of IT services ensuring that both the cloud service provider and the customer have the same definition of an acceptable level of service.

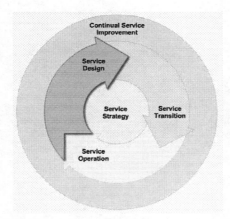

Figure 6-5: *The Service Design phase within the Service Lifecycle.*

Example: Analyzing Hard Costs and Soft Costs in Service Design

Jamie is an analyst for Rudison Technologies, which sells and supports human resources software to help keep track of employee performance. He is currently working on a project to help clients resolve errors when they call the company's help line, and he is currently attempting to quantify the costs of having the call center go offline, which has happened in the past. This analysis has both hard costs, such as money lost from unsatisfied customers taking their business to a competitor, and soft costs, such as a public relations hit. The risk of these costs should be carefully studied while the help line service is being designed, or redesigned, in this case. Jamie is designing a Service Desk with the appropriate availability for the customer to perceive value in the service.

Service Transition

Definition:

Service Transition is a phase in the Service Lifecycle that utilizes various processes, systems, and functions in order to build, test, and deploy the service before it moves into Service Operation, which is the first time a customer will see or use the service. Service Transition encompasses everything from change management to damage control to ensure that once the new cloud service has been implemented, it adheres to the given standards specified in an organization. The Change management process ensures that the standard revisions are applied to new or updated cloud services in the production level. Service Asset and Configuration Management acts as a centralized storehouse of information about the IT services and resources, including information on third party and cloud vendors.

Many cloud providers make scheduled and unscheduled releases to their offerings on a regular basis. It is essential to manage these new releases with your customers as the user interface, service functionality, and underlying integrations can change at any point. The Knowledge Management process ensures that each service provides the right level of support to organizations' users to facilitate informed decisions. For cloud computing, it is vital that cloud suppliers provide online information to all the services they support.

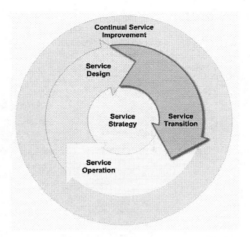

Figure 6-6: *The Service Transition within the Service Lifecycle.*

Example: Service Transition in Practice

Francis's role in the Service Transition phase of his company's current project involves managing the movement from the 0.9 beta version of the software to the major release of version 1.0. All of his efforts are focused on creating the highly detailed strategy to move from 0.9 to 1.0. This includes assigning roles to the team members, performing all necessary internal and external testing, establishing performance baselines, defining what will go into the final release as a service, and more.

Service Operations

Definition:

Service Operation is a phase in the IT Service Lifecycle where the service is first made available to customers. Service Operation has its own processes and functions that are required for the service to be provided at the agreed-upon service level.

Once the service is in operation within the cloud environment, it has to be carefully monitored to ensure that it meets the agreed levels of service. A service desk can be used to accomplish this task and achieve a high incident resolution rate. In cloud computing, the emphasis is more on identifying core issues that cause incident, and eliminating them using problem management. Customers and users must have a reliable source for any IT requests they make, so that the cloud supplier can fulfill any requests submitted to them.

Other Service Operation functions include:

● Access management to provide an extra blanket of security for secure cloud computing.

● Event management to identify alerts and their corrective actions with each cloud supplier, and then predefine the appropriate actions to resolve and remove alerts.

● Technical management to ensure that all knowledge and technical resources are available to support the IT infrastructure in place.

● IT operation management ensures that all tasks are performed according to the specifications provided.

● Application management is designed to manage all the applications that are present in the organization.

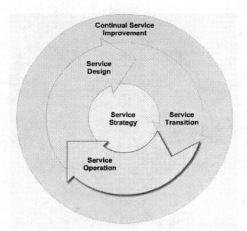

Figure 6-7: The Service Operation phase within the Service Lifecycle.

Example: Service Operation in Practice

Robert is a Project Manager for Rudison Technologies, a technological services company with a small but growing international customer base. Version 1.0 of their newest software application has been released, and they have already heard from a customer who discovered a defect. Robert's job now is to define the priority of this issue: it might be that, even with the risk of other clients using the same software, this error is unlikely to appear again. In that case, the urgency is quite low, and this incident does not threaten to have much impact on Rudison's business.

Continual Service Improvement

Definition:

Continual Service Improvement is a larger, all-encompassing phase in the IT Service Lifecycle, and is a phase that can be applied at any point in the Lifecycle. Measurement is vitally important to this phase, as it is extremely difficult to improve processes if it is not possible to identify their strengths and weaknesses. Continual service improvement is just that: continual. The work here is iterative, and is never finished. Improvements can always be made, and stages can be made more profitable.

In the continual service improvement phase, it is essential for managers to measure and analyze the performance in relation to the overall vision of the organization against its current performance levels. In this phase:

- The 7-Step Improvement process initiates the collection of hard data about performance gaps, and makes tangible reports for improvements.

- The Service Measurement Framework defines what information should be gathered, and then goes about collecting the data.

- The Service Reporting process supports building on the data-gathering activities with action plans designed to improve service and avoid known performance issues.

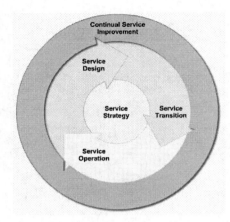

Figure 6-8: *The continual service improvement in the Service Lifecycle.*

Example: CSI and a Baseline

Rudison Technologies is a company with a mix of both on-site and off-site employees. The off-site employees connect to the company network via a Virtual Private Network (VPN). Recently, the company has decided that it wants to improve its response time for those service requests originating from the off-site employees. Greg, one of the IT managers, decides that he needs a baseline to establish what the current response time is, before he can even start planning on how to improve it.

ACTIVITY 6-1
Identifying the Phases of the Service Lifecycle

Scenario:

In this activity, you will discuss the phases of the Service Lifecycle.

---

1. **Which Lifecycle phase is concerned with building and testing a service before it is delivered to the customers?**

   a) Service Design

   b) Service Operation

   c) Service Transition

   d) Continual Service Improvement

---

2. **Which Lifecycle phase is concerned with financial planning?**

   a) Service Design

   b) Service Strategy

   c) Service Operation

   d) Service Planning

---

3. **Which phase is a larger, all-encompassing phase in the IT Service Lifecycle that can be applied at any point in the Lifecycle?**

   a) Service Transition

   b) Service Measurement

   c) Service Design

   d) Continual Service Improvement

---

4. **Which Lifecycle phase consists of processes and functions that are required for the service to be provided at the agreed-upon service level?**

   a) Service Design

   b) Service Operation

   c) Service Transition

   d) Service Strategy

TOPIC B
Planning Service Strategy

There are three key processes involved in the Service Strategy phase of the IT Service Management Lifecycle. However, before delving into them, it is important to familiarize yourself with the key concepts at the core of those processes. This topic will provide a foundation from which the major processes of the Service Strategy are built.

Projects do not have unlimited budgets or open-ended development time lines. You are often required to make the best use of the limited resources that are available to you, such as time, money, and equipment. The Service Strategy addresses these concerns early in the IT Services Lifecycle. The processes within this phase help you make smart decisions about which services to offer, and make the most efficient use of available resources while satisfying the demands of your customers.

Three Processes of Service Strategy

The Service Strategy is built upon three key processes.

- The Portfolio Management process is used for investment-related decisions regarding services.
- The Demand Management process helps an organization to align the provisioning of a service with the demand for a service.
- The Financial Management process helps an organization to use its monetary resources as efficiently as possible.

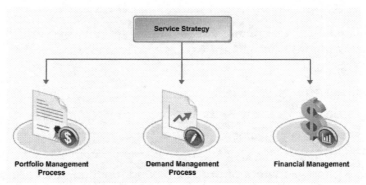

Figure 6-9: *The three processes of the Service Strategy Lifecycle phase.*

Portfolio Management

Definition:

The purpose of a *service portfolio* is to provide an overview of the types of services offered, so that they may be analyzed for investment or resource allocation purposes. Service *Portfolio Management* is a process used to make investment-related decisions across the enterprise. This practice helps service portfolio managers to identify the strengths and weaknesses of the organization in providing specific services, business requirements, and any associated costs.

Portfolio Management addresses the need to create an inventory of available services, validate their business profiles, and assign resources to support the services. It not only supports the successful adoption of cloud computing in an organization but also acts as the central repository of information accessed by cloud suppliers and cloud consumers.

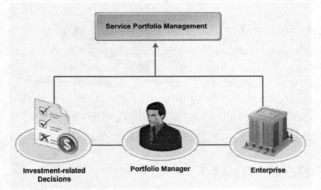

Figure 6-10: Portfolio management in an organization.

Example: High Level Business Decisions

Senior level managers at Rudison Technologies meet on a regular basis to make decisions regarding the business relationship between the service provider and its customers. Service Portfolio Management (SPM) helps managers to answer the "why" questions when it comes to services. Some questions that were brought up in the previous meetings include:

● Why should desktop support be outsourced?

● Why is this unprofitable service still in operation?

● Why should we introduce a new virtual PC service?

The senior managers are careful to keep this as a business conversation, and not a technical conversation. Discussions about technical support will be addressed later to meet the higher-level objectives discussed here.

Demand Management

Definition:

Demand Management is an essential process of the Service Strategy phase that aims to establish a balance between the offering of a service and the demand for that service. This process involves studying the amount of service consumed in a typical business activity, and being prepared to supply the necessary demand without overspending on excess capability.

Effective demand management can help an organization to accurately predict the level of product or service purchases over a specific period of time. This information is critical for capacity planning, in which the organization prepares resources in anticipation of forecasted demands. For cloud, incorrect calculation of demand will prove to be costly when there is a premium rate charged for usage over the agreed levels.

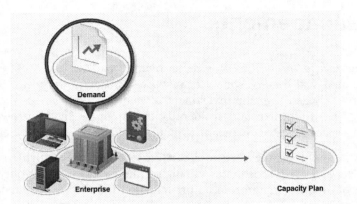

Figure 6-11: Demand management in an organization.

Example: Accommodating an Increase in Demand

The IT department at MultiCor International integrates cellular services with email, calendaring, and messaging services. The company has decided to purchase an Enterprise Server in order to bring more control of the specific PDA services in-house. MultiCor must now perform appropriate application sizing based on the number of the company's PDA users, both now and in the projected future. Since the Enterprise service is now in-sourced, the company must deliver and support the service at agreed levels.

Financial Management

The *Financial Management* process is an integrated component of Service Management that helps an organization to determine the best possible use of its monetary resources to provide services. The goal of Financial Management is to provide key decision makers within the organization with meaningful data about the financial aspects of the services offered. If implemented properly, the Financial Management process can help you determine the impact of services on revenue, the cost of the services offered, and any inefficiencies that may be encountered.

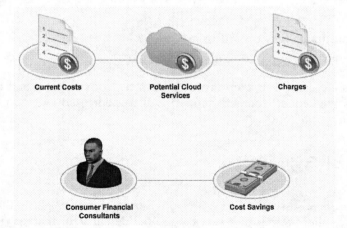

Figure 6-12: Financial management involving key decision factors in an organization.

Having an in-depth knowledge of current costs and charges will help you to analyze the projected charges for potential cloud services. It is important for consumer financial consultants to carefully evaluate, along with users, the potential costs that will benefit them with measurable cost savings.

Potential Service Strategy Risks for Cloud Computing

The three components of the Service Strategy when applied to external cloud computing help to reduce risks and maximize benefits. It is essential to identify the potential failures that an organization may encounter while adapting cloud services.

Service Strategy	Risk
Portfolio management	Failure to identify the specific delivery model of cloud will result in service delays when fixing incidents and problems. Failure to provide regulated portfolio management with clear central description of the services results in synchronization problems between the diverse IT departments who are working to adopt cloud computing. A possibility of potential contract disputes may arise in the future if the cloud suppliers are not aware of the service portfolio of the organization.
Demand management	Failure to measure the demand exactly could result in agreed demand levels going beyond the acceptable service level defined in the contracts and penalties being imposed by the cloud suppliers.
Financial management	Failure to specify and measure performance requirements during peak periods could result in unwarranted delays for users of cloud-based services.

Risks of Service Strategy

When developing your Service Strategy, it is important not to overlook potential risks. A *risk* is an uncertainty in outcome that could cause the inability to meet its objectives. It is generally measured by the likelihood of a threat, the vulnerability of an asset to that threat, and the impact the threat would have.

There are four types of risks that must be considered in the Service Strategy phase.

- Contract risks are associated with poorly negotiated agreements that may lead to difficulties in meeting service levels.
- Design risks can result from inadequacies in converting requirements to specification of the service.
- Operational risks may arise from technical or administrative failure to support the service.
- Market risks are those associated with the uncertain and increasingly competitive business environment.

How to Adopt Service Strategy for Cloud Services

Strategic goals must be defined clearly and strategic assets appropriately used to achieve business objectives. It is essential to analyze the key factors, namely risk management and risk assessment, while generating a service strategy.

Guidelines

Some of the main points that could be useful in developing a service strategy are listed for reference.

- Exceeding demand results in higher costs.
- Evaluate all the possible delivery models as a part of strategy generation.
- Difficult to bring in-house, once cloud is already implemented.
- Proper planning of staff and resources is required to avoid loss of local expertise.
- Understand the scope and limits of the cloud service.
- Adopt a traditional approach which is efficient and cheaper in comparison to the proposed cloud service.
- Consumer business managers need to be involved in the service strategy decisions.

Example: Service Strategy for Rudison Technologies

Gareth works for Rudison Technologies, which also supports IT services with antivirus programs to be installed on the customer's system. To ensure the quality of service delivery, it is important to set some strategic objectives initiating customer standards to respond to the customer effectively and efficiently. He also prepared a report by gathering feedback from the customers and recognized continuous improvement strategies to achieve the necessary results. He was able to achieve initial success and decided to expand his services by opening a branch in another state. He outsourced his services and retained the in-house facility to coordinate activities. When employing a cloud service, he verified whether the cloud provider could meet the business objectives and ensured that all contractual obligations are met by cloud services. The agreement terms were clearly defined and accepted by both users and cloud service providers. By taking a strategic approach, Gareth was able to accomplish all the business objectives of the organization.

ACTIVITY 6-2
Understanding the Fundamental Concepts of Service Strategy

Scenario:

In this activity, you will identify and explore the basic concepts of Service Strategy.

---

1. **Identify the three different phases of Service Strategy.**

    a) Portfolio Management

    b) Demand Management

    c) Change Management

    d) Financial Management

---

2. **What is the overall goal of demand management?**

    a) To determine the best possible use of its monetary resources to provide services.

    b) To determine a balance between the offering of a service and the demand for that service.

    c) To deliver and support operational IT services to achieve business and deliver forecasted business benefits.

    d) To deliver service value by facilitating the desired outcome that customers want to achieve.

---

3. **Who also should be included in making service strategy decisions along with the cloud providers?**

    a) Capacity Manager

    b) IT Staff

    c) Consumer Business Managers

    d) Security Manager

---

4. **Identify the risks that are involved in the three stages of Service Strategy.**

    a) Failure to identify the specific delivery model of cloud will result in service delays when fixing incidents and problems.

    b) Failure to provide services and meet demands ahead of time.

    c) Failure to measure the demand exactly could result in agreed demand levels going beyond and penalties being imposed by the cloud suppliers.

    d) Failure to specify and measure performance requirements during peak periods could result in unwarranted delays for users of cloud-based services.

TOPIC C
Designing Cloud Service

It has been said that early preparation can save time and money down the road. This principle lends itself to the IT Service Lifecycle as well as Cloud services. In this topic, you will describe the basic concepts of Service Design that are useful in the groundwork for the underlying processes that will run the new cloud services.

The Service Design phase cannot be approached with a cookie-cutter mentality. Different clients may require different services, or different levels of a similar service. To create cloud services that meet or exceed customer expectations, you must be able to understand the aspects of the service design, as well as the various delivery options. Doing so helps you to match your services with your clients in the most efficient manner possible.

The Service Catalog

Definition:

The *service catalog* consists of all active and approved services that a provider currently offers to its client base. Services within the catalog are divided into components, each containing policies and guidelines that document any applicable SLAs and delivery conditions.

Example: Service Catalog vs. Service Portfolio

Rudison Technologies employs a Service Desk that provides support for end users. Information regarding all proprietary applications used by the company is included within the IT department's service catalog. However, support for a legacy content management system has been discontinued within the past year. This would be categorized as a retired service within the overall service portfolio.

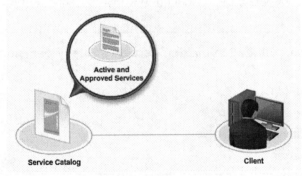

Figure 6-13: The service catalog is a component of the service portfolio.

Service Catalog Management

Definition:

Service Catalog Management (SCM) is the practice of maintaining an organization's service catalog. It usually contains any information relevant to the details, status, upkeep, and interactions of all current operational services, as well as those that are in consideration. The services include both cloud services and other operational services such as internal services and outsourced services. It is essential that proper planning is done to ensure that new cloud services will integrate with current services and there is no usage of unauthorized cloud services to avoid extra costs and possibly other contractual penalties.

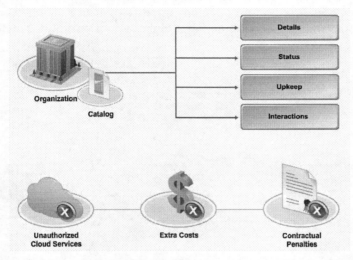

Figure 6-14: *The service catalog management with cloud operations in an organization.*

Example: Managing a Service Catalog

The Service Desk at Rudison Technologies provides IT services for end users. Currently, information about each service, including SLAs, support hours, contact numbers, and more, is part of its service catalog. The department is auditing the service catalog to ensure that it correctly reflects all of the live services as well as those services ready to be delivered to customers.

Distinction between Service Catalog and Service Portfolio

The distinction between a service catalog and a service portfolio is sometimes unclear. The service catalog represents only a portion of the overall service portfolio, albeit the most substantial portion. The service portfolio consists of all current services, all pipeline services that are in consideration or in planning or development, and all retired services that are no longer supported.

Activities of SCM

The service catalog is a centralized resource for all parties who are involved with providing or receiving an organization's services. Successful SCM includes activities such as:

● Clearly defining the services offered.

● Maintaining the service catalog and making it available.

● Keeping stakeholders up-to-date about the service catalog.

● Managing the interaction and dependencies of services within the overall portfolio.

● Monitoring the *Configuration Management System (CMS)*.

Service Level Management

Definition:

Service Level Management is the process responsible for negotiating *Service Level Agreements, Operational Level Agreements, Underpinning Contracts (SLAs, OLAs, UCs)* and ensuring that the agreed upon service levels are met by cloud suppliers. The primary function of Service Level Management is to provide a framework for the delivery of IT services and to set the expectations of service quality that is delivered to customers. These requirements are essential in ensuring that both the cloud service provider and the customer have the same definition of an acceptable level of service.

Another function of Service Level Management is to monitor the service for quality and take corrective actions as necessary to close any gaps in performance. Regular reviews are essential in maintaining customer relations and retaining a high level of customer satisfaction.

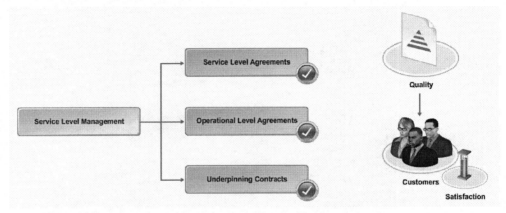

Figure 6-15: Service Level Management comprising other sub agreements.

Example: Service Level Management at LearnMark

Ristell Prints is a small printer and copier service company with dozens of clients in a medium-sized metropolitan area. Within the Service Design phase, the Service Level Management process aims to ensure that all negotiated service levels with the customer are being met. Even if the level of service being provided is satisfactory, the goal of Service Level Management is to proactively seek ways to improve the level of service being offered through regular monitoring, reporting, and adjusting.

Types of Agreement

There are three different types of agreements between IT and customers.

Agreement	Description
Service Level Agreement (SLA)	A SLA is a documented agreement between a service provider and a customer that fully describes the service, and specifies the responsibilities of both the provider and the customer. An SLA may be applicable to multiple IT services or to multiple customers. The planning, coordinating, monitoring, and reporting of these SLAs is the heart of the Service Level Management process.

Agreement	Description
Operational Level Agreement (OLA)	An Operational Level Agreement (OLA) is an internal agreement between the functions within the IT service provider. This agreement is noncontractual, and therefore is not legally binding. The goal of the OLA is to establish the level of support required for different functions within the IT service provider to satisfy the SLA targets that were promised to their customers. In essence, an OLA defines what the IT service provider must do internally in order to allow other areas of the business to serve its clients.
Underpinning Contracts (UC)	A contract is a legally binding agreement among two or more entities. A contract may be between a service provider and a supplier, a service provider and a customer, or among all three. The contract clearly outlines the conditions and expectations of each party involved, and typically includes expectations of services, compensation for services, time constraints, and terms of usage. Failure on any side to comply with the conditions in a contract may result in legal action.

Service Level Requirement (SLR)

A Service Level Requirement (SLR) is a specific customer requirement for an aspect of the service. It is based on the customer's specific business needs that are necessary for the customers to meet their own objectives. This is a critical part of the Service Level Management negotiation, as different customers will likely have different specific demands for a service. For instance, a five-second delay in a streaming voice application has a greater business impact than the same delay in loading a web page.

Availability Management

Definition:

Availability Management is the process responsible for ensuring that the IT infrastructure, processes, tools, and roles that utilize the cloud are available and appropriate for the agreed-upon service level targets. The goal of Availability Management is to establish acceptable levels of availability, monitor the services to ensure that these levels are met, and then make any improvements as needed to processes and equipment.

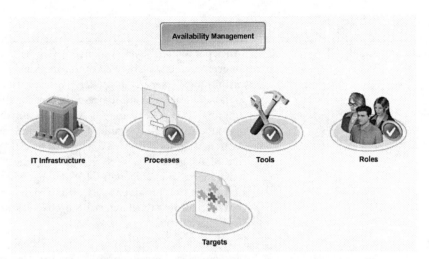

Figure 6-16: Availability Management with its various functions in an organization.

Example: Email Uptime Agreement

A service provider has promised 99.9% uptime for an email system in an SLA. The service provider and the customer agree that the email system will be down for maintenance for two hours once a week, beginning at 2 AM on Sunday morning. Any downtime other than this planned two-hour window is to be tracked and diagnosed.

Five Nines Availability

The uptime and availability of a particular system is most often measured in nines, such as 99% or 99.9%. "Five Nines" is a term used to describe a specific level of high availability, which is 99.999% uptime. To get an understanding of how difficult Five Nines availability is to achieve, it allows for only 5 minutes and 35 seconds of downtime over an entire year, which is just 6 seconds of downtime per week. The reason that availability is measured in nines is because it is assumed that 100% availability is unachievable. Instead, you can only strive to achieve as many "nines" as possible.

High Availability

As businesses become more reliant upon the constant availability of IT services, there is an increased demand for highly available solutions. *High availability* is an approach to IT service design that aims to remove single points of failure (SPOFs) from the architecture, so that the failure of a specific device will have as minimal an effect as possible. High availability often uses technologies such as fault tolerance, resilience, and fast recovery to limit the amount of interruptions to the service, and then reduce the amount of time required to restore that service if other precautions are unable to prevent an interruption.

Capacity Management

Definition:

Capacity Management is the process responsible for ensuring that the capacity of IT services meets expected levels of service performance, while keeping costs within the budget. Finding the optimum level of capacity is not an easy task. The usage levels of an IT service or cloud service vary on a daily basis, and will likely change over time. In addition, an increase in capacity is typically accompanied by an increase in costs.

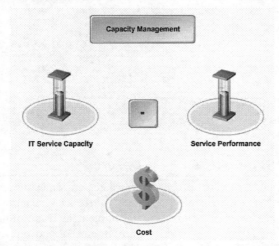

Figure 6-17: Capacity management determining the optimum capacity requirements.

The goal of Capacity Management is to leverage the current needs of the business with the anticipated future needs. This requires insightful analyses of future trends and requirements, and involves careful planning to ensure that all required resources can be provisioned cost effectively, and cloud suppliers do not incur financial penalties.

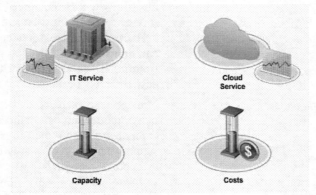

Figure 6-18: Capacity management for cloud services deployed in an organization.

Example: Balancing the Present and Future

In revisiting the VoIP capacity issue at Rudison Technologies, it is clear to the IT Service Desk that changes need to be made to the infrastructure in order to accommodate the increased usage of web conferencing. However, meeting current demands will only address the problem for now. Effective Capacity Management should factor in not just the demands of today, but also the demands of tomorrow. As resources are limited, smart decisions must be made about where resources can produce the greatest gain.

Types of Capacity Management

Capacity Management is a complex process that utilizes three key subprocesses.

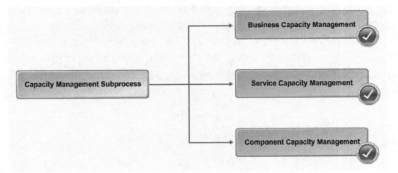

Figure 6-19: Capacity Management Subprocess.

Capacity Management Subprocess	Description
Business Capacity Management	Translates customer requirements into specifications for the IT service, which are to be designed and implemented in a timely fashion. The focus is on both current and future needs. This is about the throughput required by the business processes and really doesn't have anything to do with IT. For example, this is the difference between a bank that processes 10 loan applications a day and a bank that processes 100 loan applications a day.
Service Capacity Management	Identifies the performance of the operational IT service in order to ensure that the performance meets or exceeds the agreed upon level. The IT service capacity must be sufficient to support the business capacity requirements. For example, the bank must receive the appropriate service levels from its IT service provider to underwrite loans at desired levels of demand.
Component Capacity Management	Manages and predicts the performance of each individual technology component to ensure that all components within the infrastructure are able to support the service capacity that is required. For example, the server running the loan application software must keep up with the demand for that service as offered to customers of the IT service provider.

IT Service Continuity Management

Definition:

IT Service Continuity Management is the process that supports the overall business continuity management (BCM) process by establishing a framework, which ensures that interruptions in an IT service or a cloud service are resolved within agreed-upon time frames. It involves managing a business's ability to continue to deliver a predetermined level of service following a critical interruption to that service. It is essential to monitor the web for cloud failures and to check with the current cloud suppliers to ensure that they have the appropriate protection in place.

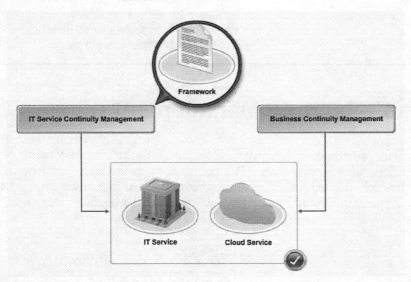

Figure 6-20: IT service continuity addresses disastrous outages.

Example: Planning for the Unplanned

Hexa Web Hosting Services has an SLA with its customer base that a specific web application will be provided 24 hours a day. To avoid the service outages that would result from a catastrophic power failure, the business has a backup power generator that is capable of powering the servers that run this application until the main power is restored. This represents one component of Hexa's overall IT Service Continuity Management process.

Types of Continuity

IT Service Continuity Management typically defines different levels of continuity for different time frames following the interruption.

Recovery Type	Description
Immediate	Known as "Hot." This includes immediate actions taken to restore a service, typically involving site mirroring or hot swapping.
Fast	Known as "Hot." This includes actions taken to restore a service within 24 hours of failure, which may involve data replication from other operational servers.

Recovery Type	Description
Intermediate	Known as "Warm." This includes actions taken to restore a service within 24 to 72 hours of failure. This generally involves maintaining computing equipment, and occurs after the restoration of critical data and/or application services.
Gradual	Known as "Cold." This includes actions taken that require more than 72 hours to restore a service. Gradual recovery typically entails any changes to facilities or processes that may provide further defenses against interruptions or improve recovery capabilities.

Information Security Management

Definition:

Information Security Management is a process that involves the overall security of an organization's assets, information, and services. The concerns of Information Security Management extend beyond the technical aspects of system access controls, infrastructure, and service vulnerabilities. It includes policies and procedures that protect the business from both external and internal security breaches.

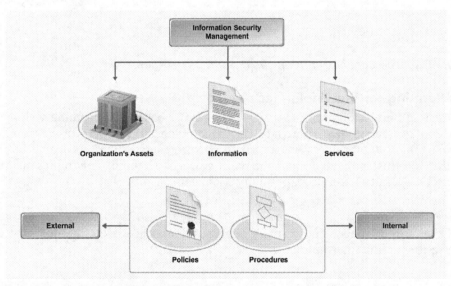

Figure 6-21: *Information Security Management in an organization.*

Effective Information Security Management also protects the business from legal issues. For traditional IT services and the cloud environment, customer data, especially that of external clients, is very sensitive and must be protected as part of the information confidentiality agreement. Regular checks should be planned to ensure the service management is resilient to security breaches.

Example: Employee Data

The HR department at Rudison Technologies stores very sensitive data about every employee in a database. It is critical that only certain staff members have access to this information. The IT Service Desk must ensure that the policies are enforced to categorize employees based on their role in the organization, and that only authorized personnel, such as HR staff, can view this specific information. Personal data such as Social Security numbers, salaries, and home addresses should not be made accessible to other employees.

The IT Security Framework

The *Information Security Management System (ISMS)* is a framework of policies, processes, standards, guidelines, and tools that ensure that an organization can achieve its Information Security Management objectives. This standard represents the foundation for the development of information security policies centered on the 4 Ps—people, processes, products, and partners. The ISMS framework also provides information about five specific elements—control, plan, implement, evaluate, and maintain—and outlines their individual objectives.

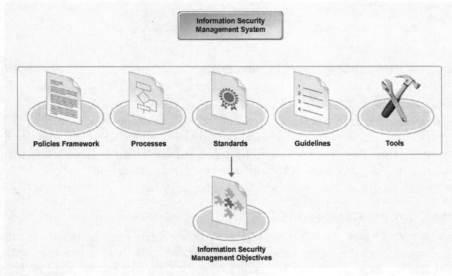

Figure 6-22: The framework for managing IT security.

Supplier Management

Definition:

A supplier is any external party who plays a role in the ability of a service provider to offer a service to a customer. *Supplier Management* is the process by which suppliers are overseen to ensure that the services they provide are sufficient so that the IT service provider or the cloud provider is able to fulfill its obligations to its own customers.

Contractual obligations between the cloud supplier and the service provider must be met in order for the service provider to render their own services. For cloud computing when there are multiple cloud providers, it is essential to manage the external cloud suppliers as part of an internal IT team within your organization so that they maintain and follow established policies and processes to ensure consistent delivery of IT services. It is also vital to verify the validity of a contract signed for external cloud suppliers because a legal contract in one country may not be considered legal in another country.

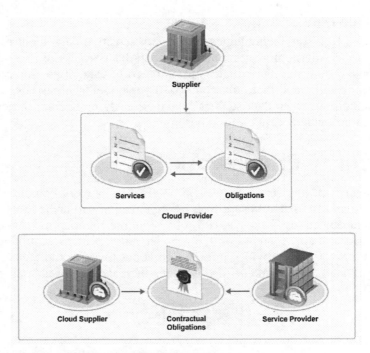

Figure 6-23: The supplier management infrastructure.

Example: Selecting a Supplier

Rudison Technologies wants to offer a service that allows clients to access remote PCs so that they can perform configurations in a simulated environment. Since these devices are located off-site, Rudison requires that the devices be hosted and maintained by an outside supplier. The company carefully investigates a pool of available suppliers to determine who is best suited to meet the business demands at the most favorable cost.

Supplier and Contract Database (SCD)

Supplier and Contract Database (SCD) is a database that contains all the pertinent information regarding all suppliers and their contracts, along with the details that outline the type of services rendered and the expected levels of quality of each. The success of supplier management depends on developing and maintaining sound policies with the suppliers. These policies can be made consistent and effective through the creation of the SCD.

Specialized Roles of the Service Design Phase

There are also specialized roles for overseeing each of the seven processes in Service Design.

Specialized Role	Description
Service Level Manager	**Process:** Service Level Management **Responsibility:** Oversees the negotiations and management of Service Level Agreements (SLAs), and ensures that they are met or exceeded.

Specialized Role	Description
Service Catalog Manager	**Process:** Service Catalog Management **Responsibility:** Ensures that the service catalog is maintained, contains the most current information, and is available to all stakeholders.
Availability Manager	**Process:** Availability Management **Responsibility:** Ensures that the service meets or exceeds all customer availability requirements as described in the SLA.
Capacity Manager	**Process:** Capacity Management **Responsibility:** Balances resources and costs so that the level of service is acceptable for users both now and in the future.
Security Manager	**Process:** Information Security Management **Responsibility:** Defends the security of the organization's assets, information, and services.
Service Continuity Manager	**Process:** IT Service Continuity Management **Responsibility:** Ensures that any critical interruptions to a service are resolved within a specific time frame.
Supplier Manager	**Process:** Supplier Management **Responsibility:** Manages relationships with all suppliers and ensures that their levels of service are sufficient for the organization to provide its own services.

Service Design Considerations

The Service Design phase in the ITIL Lifecycle aims to provide guidance to designing IT services and facilitating their implementation into the live environment, ensuring quality service delivery, customer satisfaction, and cost-effective service provision.

Guidelines

Some key points that may be relevant for cloud implementation are listed for reference.

- Service Level Agreements, Operational Level Agreements, and Underpinning contracts should be clearly defined, understood, and agreed upon between the users and cloud providers for the governance of cloud services.

- Service Level Management should be effective so as to monitor, measure, report, and review the level of IT services provided to the customer and that they meet their agreed level of service.

- Highlight all the potential operational issues that may arise as a result of the new cloud services and plan the service catalog to meet the new cloud requirements.

- Avoid unauthorized cloud usage by updating service catalog regularly and ensuring that customers are using the cloud services that they are only entitled to.

- Necessary tools should be available to validate whether the cloud suppliers meet their contractual obligations.

- Ownership of data issues should be avoided and legal cloud contracts with the cloud suppliers should be checked by international lawyers.
- Identify all the potential threats and monitor the security breaches for external cloud computing applications.
- Identify the service continuity requirements for external cloud applications and review and update them whenever required.
- Regular analysis should be performed to ensure that capacity level meets the planned growth criteria.
- Measurement tools should be installed to manage and monitor the usage of the available resources within the agreed usage level.

Example: Service Design in Practice

Cindy worked as a project manager for an airport reservation system, and wanted to compete against the stiff market competition. Cindy developed a team and identified the crucial insights. She identified common complaints from customers about long lines and the inability to make reservations from home at their own convenience. They developed an online system and offered various services where the customers could book tickets online, through mobile or through other resources including the local agents. They ensured that the customer is kept updated of his current status and the online system is regularly monitored to avoid any potential threat. If seats are available, the wait-listed tickets will be confirmed automatically; otherwise, tickets will be cancelled with money being refunded to them through their respective method of payment. This process proved to be successful and continual service improvements are considered to provide improved customer satisfaction.

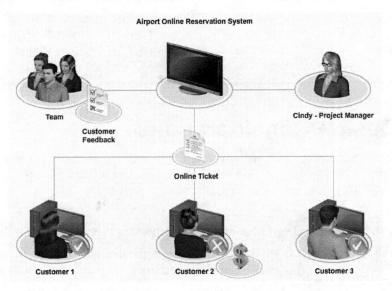

Figure 6-24: Service Design in Practice.

Impact of Poor Cloud Service Design

When service design is not in place, results can be disastrous for an organization. Some of the facts that are likely to occur when service design fails to deliver the required services include:

- IT services for cloud computing prove to be costlier on a day-to-day basis than the set expectations.

- The organization is unable to control the costs incurred for cloud implementation, because of the various changes resulting in poor value for money.

- IT service becomes obsolete as more focus is given on application development with a little consideration for the IT service.

- Cloud services that go into the operation phase are incomplete or incompatible.

ACTIVITY 6-3
Understanding the Service Design Lifecycle

Scenario:

In this activity, you will review the various concepts and processes of the Service Design Lifecycle phase.

1. **Match each management process with its corresponding example.**

   ___ Information Security Management

   ___ Capacity Management

   ___ Supplier Management

   ___ Availability Management

   ___ Service Catalog Management

   a. Single points of failure are removed from the infrastructure in order to add resiliency.

   b. Databases containing financial data are available to employees within the finance department only.

   c. The IT department audits its service to ensure that all documented service hours, contact numbers, and Service Level Agreements (SLAs) are correct.

   d. The number of users for this service is expected to double over the next two years.

   e. A plan is put into place for an Internet service provider (ISP) whose performance was below expectations last quarter.

2. **Which of the following is an internal agreement between the support teams of an IT service provider?**

   a) Department Support Agreement

   b) Service Level Agreement

   c) IT Support Agreement

   d) Operational Level Agreement

3. **True or False? The ability of an organization to restore Service Operations after a catastrophic failure is the goal of availability management.**

   ___ True

   ___ False

4. **Samuel establishes a formal agreement with a client to set up the service hours of operation, transaction response times, and throughput expectations. This activity is part of which process of the Service Design Phase?**

    a) Availability Management

    b) Capacity Management

    c) Service Level Management

    d) Supplier Management

TOPIC D
Transitioning to Live Environment

Now that you have designed and developed the services in the Service Design phase, it is important to understand how to properly manage changes to your services so that the perception of value is not lost. Therefore, it is important to deliver the changes that your customers require in an efficient and effective manner. In this topic, you will describe the Service Transition Lifecycle phase.

IT services never get deployed permanently; the world of IT services is constantly changing, as new technologies are developed and older ones being deprecated, and existing contracts with providers end with new ones taking their place. Customers will never want to see their services interrupted while you make your transition. Therefore, understanding how to adapt, change, and improve cloud services that go from testing to deployment is critical for continued, smooth operation.

Service Transition Processes

The scope of the Service Transition phase involves the coordination of six different processes.

- The Change Management process ensures that all changes are implemented in a standardized manner. Changes must be evaluated, prioritized, approved, tested, and documented before being made available to users.

- Service Asset and Configuration Management (SACM) establishes control over the physical IT infrastructure by defining all configuration items and maintaining configuration records in a centralized place.

- Release and Deployment Management oversees the building, testing, and delivering of the services, and determines the best way to deploy new releases to the user base.

- Knowledge Management aims to improve both the speed and quality of decision making by aggregating knowledge previously dispersed across the organization into a central location that can be accessed by anyone who needs it.

- Service Validation and Testing aims to prove that the new/changed service is able to support the business objectives, including the agreed upon SLAs.

- Evaluation ensures that the service is relevant and extends support by establishing appropriate metrics and measurement techniques.

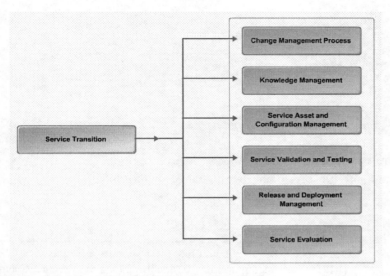

Figure 6-25: *Service Transition with various subprocesses.*

Change Management

Definition:

Change Management is a process which ensures that changes are deployed in a standardized manner. This process oversees the evaluation, prioritization, planning, testing, implementation, and documentation of change requests. The change management process does not guarantee that changes made to IT services will not cause any problems. Rather, the goal of change management is to minimize the risks involved in making changes, while adding the greatest amount of value. In a cloud environment, it is important that all parties involved in the change or affected by the change be notified and security breach be monitored to prevent any unlawful criminal activities.

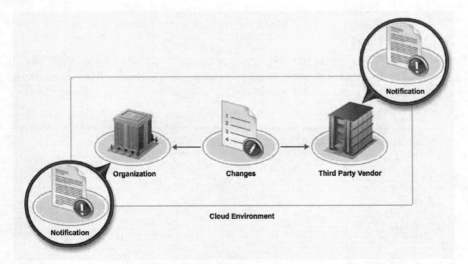

Figure 6-26: *The change management process with cloud services deployed in an organization.*

Example:

Figure 6-27: The change management process.

Activities of Change Management

There are seven key activities associated with change management.

Activity	Description
Create and record	The process begins when a requestor submits a Request for Change (RFC). This document must be identifiable, and is recorded and logged.
Review the request	The request is investigated by the members of the IT Service Desk or other stakeholders. The RFC is reviewed to make sure that it is logical, feasible, complete, and has not already been submitted.
Assess the change	The Change Manager or *CAB* determines whether the change should be made. This decision is based on the impact of the change, a risk analysis, and a cost-benefit analysis.
Authorize the change	Provided that the RFC meets all criteria, it receives formal authorization. Authorization often reflects the amount of risk it entails.
Plan the change	*Remediation* planning should be conducted in order to explicitly address the issue of what to do if the change is unsuccessful.
Coordinate implementation	Once the change request is approved, the coordination begins. The actual work is completed during the release and deployment process, which begins at this point. The details and requirements of the change are forwarded to experts, who then build, test, and deploy the change.
Review and close	The implemented change is evaluated after being rolled out. This evaluation process seeks to ensure that the change has met its objectives and has not introduced any problems. If all is well, it can be closed.

Service Asset and Configuration Management

Definition:

Service Asset and Configuration Management (SACM) is the process responsible for managing both service assets and all configuration items (CI). The goal of SACM is to establish control over the physical IT infrastructure by defining infrastructure components and maintaining configuration records.

Asset Management covers the inventory of assets from acquisition to disposal, and deals with the value and depreciation of those assets. *Configuration Management* aims to account for, manage, and protect the integrity of CIs required to deliver an IT service, as well as their relationships to other CIs.

In the cloud environment, configuration management defines a relationship between local traceable CIs and remote cloud components and integrates them to ensure that all the changes and upgrades are performed smoothly. Cloud suppliers need to have their own CIs in the *Configuration Management Data Base* (CMDB) so that they are integrated in the local CMDB for planning, change, and risk assessments purposes.

Example:

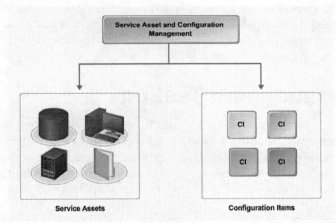

Figure 6-28: *Service Asset and Configuration Management managing service assets and all configuration items (CI).*

Release and Deployment Management

Definition:

To understand the release and deployment management process, you must be able to draw a distinction between the two terms. A *release* is a collection of new configuration items that are tested and implemented. A release can be a combination of hardware, software, processes, or other components that are required to enable or enhance an IT service. *Deployment* is the activity responsible for migrating the new release to the live environment.

The *release and deployment management* process oversees the building, testing, and delivering of the services that are identified in the Service Design phase of the lifecycle. The process ensures that customers can use the new or modified cloud service in a way that supports business objectives. Once a new release is deployed on the web, all users of that software will automatically use the new release as soon as they load or refresh the software. Assurance is provided by cloud suppliers that the cloud-resident software removes many of the obstacles associated with rollouts and deployment.

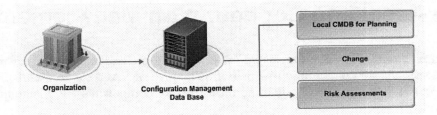

Figure 6-29: *Release and deployment management process.*

Example: New Software Release

Ristell & Sons Publishing creates web-hosted content through proprietary authoring software. In response to the changing demands for improved functionality and commonly used features, the IT staff has prepared a new release of the software. The new version must be built and thoroughly tested before it can be deployed to the user base. The release and deployment management process will oversee the development, testing, and rollout of the new release in order to minimize the trouble of upgrading and getting users accustomed to the new version.

Release Management

Release management ensures that the services scheduled for release are tested for quality assurance before their deployment in the live environment. In this process all services deployed for release are organized, integrated and tested before their release. It is one of the integral parts of the release and deployment management process.

Service Validation and Testing

Service Validation and Testing involves testing all the services, whether in-house or through external cloud suppliers, and providing validation so that business objectives can be met according to the expectations and contractual obligations defined in the service portfolio. When selecting a cloud service supplier, it is critical to focus on choosing the best service provider so that they match the client requirements and provide the services and functions required by users.

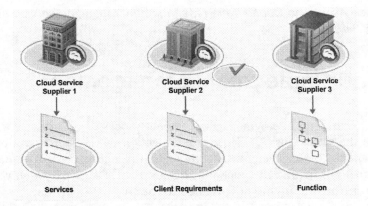

Figure 6-30: *Service validation and testing process in an organization.*

Service Evaluation

Service Evaluation ensures that all services are relevant to the success of the business by establishing appropriate metrics and measurement techniques. In a nutshell, it considers the suitability of the new or changed service for the actual operational and business environments encountered and expected. When these changes occur in a remote or virtual cloud environment, IT needs to perform its role and evaluate the predicted outcome of a change against the actual outcome of a change. This is done to ensure that there is no potential fallout, and cloud changes do not result in negative effects.

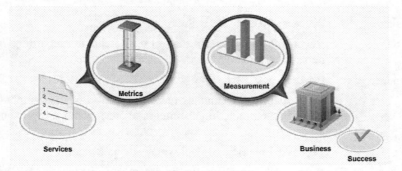

Figure 6-31: Service evaluation with various metrics in a cloud infrastructure.

Knowledge Management

Definition:

Knowledge Management is the process by which data is gathered, analyzed, stored, and shared across an entire organization. A major factor for the success of the Service Transition phase is the speed at which quality decisions can be made regarding IT services. When dispersed data across the organization is centralized in one location, appropriate information can be made available to the right people at the right time. This centralization of data allows the expertise of all staff to be combined so that any information and knowledge acquired can be shared with other personnel for future reference.

Example: Known Issue Knowledge Sharing

Employees at Rudison Technologies have been using a new version of the content publishing system for about three months. As more and more users become familiar with the program, the list of known issues with the program grows. Many users are able to find workarounds for these issues. The IT Service Desk creates an internal database of known issues and solutions for these roadblocks, so that users who are just learning the program can find a quick answer to a problem instead of relearning a known fix.

Specialized Roles of the Service Transition Phase

In addition to the generic roles of the Service Transition phase, there are roles that correspond to specific processes within the phase.

Specialized Role	Description
Change Manager	**Process:** Change management **Responsibility:** Ensures that the changes are evaluated, prioritized, and deployed in a controlled manner.
Configuration Manager	**Process:** SACM **Responsibility:** Ensures that all documentation regarding configuration items is updated.
Service Asset Manager	**Process:** SACM **Responsibility:** Maintains records about all of the company's service assets, which include information about inventory levels and the worth of all assets.
Deployment Manager	**Process:** Release and deployment management **Responsibility:** Oversees the planning and execution of the deployment of new releases for configuration items. Determines the best method of making releases available to the user base.
Risk-Evaluation Manager	**Process:** Change management, release and deployment management **Responsibility:** Determines and evaluates the risks of introducing a change, as well as any risks posed by integrating a new release into the live environment.
Service Knowledge Manager	**Process:** Knowledge management **Responsibility:** Coordinates the collection, organization, and availability of all the organization's knowledge sources.

How to Transition to Cloud

The Service Transition phase in the ITIL Lifecycle aims to provide guidance for the development of capabilities for the transition of new and changed services into operations, ensuring that they meet the service strategy requirements encoded in the service design package. They are effectively realized in Service Operations while controlling the risks of failure and disruption.

Guidelines

Some key points that may be relevant for cloud implementation are listed.

- Business users should be informed of the risks and potential impacts before the change takes place.
- Informed changes will lead to better planning and implementation of services with minimal disruption to the business.
- Service fails if the initial shortfalls are not identified until late in the operation phase.
- Frequent cloud outages occur when IT services fail to perform as expected.
- Services get delayed and they cause a security threat to the cloud customers.
- IT services run out of capacity often resulting in inflated unexpected cost.

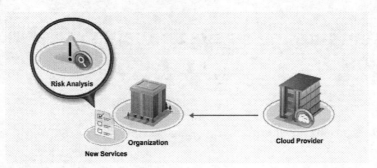

Figure 6-32: *Service transition process in an organization.*

Example: IT Transition at Hexa Web Services

Hexa Web Services create anti-virus content through proprietary software. For improved functionality and commonly used features, the IT staff has prepared a new release of the software. The new version must be built and thoroughly tested before it can be deployed to the user base. The release and deployment management process will oversee the development, testing, and rollout of the new release in order to minimize the trouble of upgrading and getting the users accustomed to the new version. Key stakeholders are informed about the guidelines required for the anti-virus software.

ACTIVITY 6-4
Understanding the Basic Concepts of Service Transition

Scenario:
In this activity, you will discuss the basic concepts of the Service Transition phase.

1. **Which of the following is an objective of the Service Transition phase?**

    a) To develop strategies on what the business needs, and what it does not.

    b) To develop a strategy for restoring normal service operation as quickly as possible following a disruption.

    c) To continually realign IT services to changing business needs.

    d) To plan and manage the resources to establish a new or changed service into production within constraints.

2. **Which of the following processes of the Service Transition phase manages the building, testing, and delivering of new or changed service components?**

    a) Change management

    b) SACM

    c) Release and deployment management

    d) Knowledge management

TOPIC E
Running a Cloud Service Operation

Before getting into the details of the Service Operation Lifecycle phase, there are some key terms that you need to become familiar with. By learning these terms now, you will be better prepared to see how the various processes of the Service Operation phase actually work, what they have in common with one another, and how they differ. In this topic, you will describe some basic concepts of Service Operation.

Service Operation requires that you work closely with people who might not always share your knowledge base. You will be communicating with other members of your company, and you will need to help coordinate the large effort of supporting, studying, and maintaining an IT service used by customers. In order to keep the service running smoothly, you will need to know how to talk to the other participants in this phase and during this process, even if you all do not share the same job role. By understanding the basic concepts of Service Operation, you can better prepare yourself for whatever process you need to participate in, and for communicating with other team members as you support IT services.

Service Desk

Definition:

A *service desk* is a single point of contact between users and the service provider that attempts to restore normal service to users as quickly as possible. A service desk typically manages incidents, service requests, and access requests, and also handles communication with users.

For cloud-based deployment models, most of the technology and the knowledge to support those cloud services reside in an external environment and users need access to knowledge resources to perform those cloud services. It is important for the service desk to carefully and continually monitor the performance and observe the quality of service provided by in-house knowledge resources and cloud service desk.

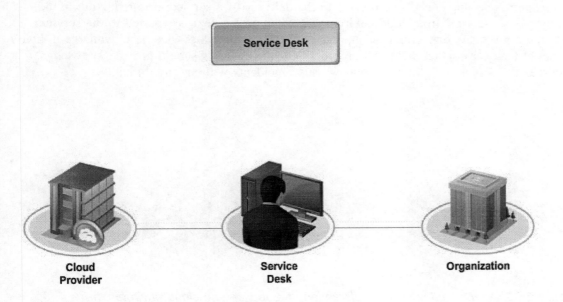

Figure 6-33: Service Desk function in an organization

Example: Service Desk Operations

To resolve an issue, the in-house service desk should support the complete knowledge resource about the cloud service and should be available to the user on demand. Failure to find an appropriate source will escalate the concern to the service desk who will account it as second-level support for the in-house service desk. In the case of the cloud service desk, who will be the first point of contact?

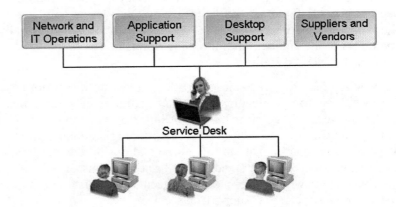

Figure 6-34: A Service Desk with various support functions in an organization.

Service Desk vs. Help Desk

ITIL draws a clear distinction between a service desk and a help desk. A *Help Desk* is a point of contact for users to log incidents, and is usually more technically focused than a service desk. However, it does not provide a single point of contact for all interaction. Although many people tend to use the terms interchangeably, the terms service desk and help desk are not synonymous.

Incident

Definition:

An *incident* is an unplanned interruption to the delivery of a service, or a reduction in the quality of that service. In a cloud environment when an incident is reported to the service desk, there are many concerns that one has to check. Is there a service desk available in-house or should the user contact the cloud provider? Cloud providers should provide knowledge resources to users so that they can manage such incidents without any difficulty.

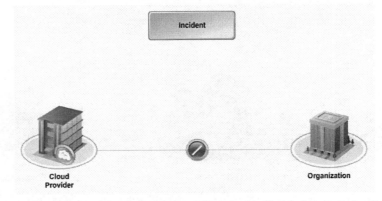

Figure 6-35: An Incident showing a disruption of a service in a cloud environment.

Example: Incidents are Disruptive

Joseph is an analyst for Ristell & Sons Publishing. He arrives at his desk one morning and discovers that his computer does not connect to the company intranet, and he finds that he is not leasing an IP address to gain access to the Internet. This disruptive incident prevents him from doing anything, including using the company database to submit a help request.

Incident Lifecycle

An *Incident Lifecycle* is a process used to analyze the time spent during each step of resolving an incident, as well as the time in between incidents. Resolving an incident includes the time taken to: detect, record, and diagnose the incident, repair the infrastructure, recover any affected components, and restore the service. An incident is identified by an event management or a user communicating to the service desk; the role of the incident lifecycle is to track and manage it. It is vital to focus on which support process will resolve the incident before moving to cloud.

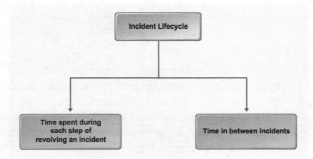

Figure 6-36: Incident Lifecycle in an organization.

Incident Management

Definition:

Incident Management is a process dedicated to the restoration of normal service as quickly as possible. Since the customer is unable to do the intended work, the goal of Incident Management is to get the service back up and running with minimal delay. When an incident is tracked in the lifecycle, an informed decision is taken about who will be the first point of contact for support—an in-house or cloud provider will resolve the incident. The primary responsibility lies within the IT service company with an established IT service management process. If it is a cloud service desk, then the cloud supplier should maintain and provide a detailed list of cloud based incidents logged to the consumers' ITSM process. This will ensure for a continual service improvement process for the delivery of the service. A common incident management tool should be available both to the cloud supplier and users where they log their incidents. This would ensure that there is complete cooperation between the user and the consumer.

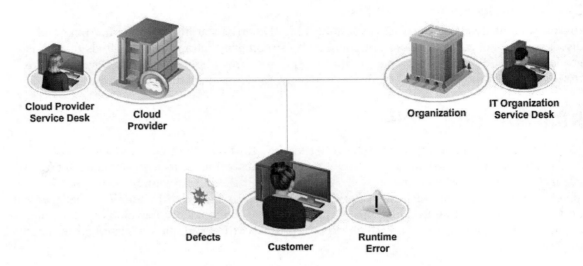

Figure 6-37: *Incident management process in an organization.*

Example: Managing an Incident

Carey logs on to her desktop after lunch and discovers that she cannot access any of the company intranet sites. After clicking around to see what has happened, she discovers that her firewall is now blocking all the intranet sites. She calls the Service Desk and has someone with proper administrative permissions delete the rule in her firewall that blocks all the internal sites. The Incident Management process is not concerned with why the error occurred, but only with the restoration of the service; in this case, intranet access.

Example: Incident Model

Quite a few incidents are not new; they have happened before, they continue to happen, and they likely will happen in the future. To expedite the process of dealing with an incident, some organizations find it helpful to create an incident model. An incident model contains:

- Any predefined steps that should be taken for dealing with a particular kind of incident.
- The order in which these steps should be executed.
- Who is responsible for what.
- The time line for completing the action.
- Any escalation advice.
- Any reason or strategies for preserving evidence.

By creating an incident model, you can ensure that any regularly occurring incidents are handled efficiently and effectively.

Activities of Incident Management

There are several activities in Incident Management.

Activity	Description
Identification	The incident is detected, or someone has reported it.
Registration	The incident record is created.
Categorization	The incident is given a type, status, impact, urgency, etc.

Activity	Description
Prioritization	The incident is given a prioritization code to manage how it gets handled by staff.
Initial Diagnosis	An initial diagnosis is performed to discover the complete symptoms of the incident. Diagnostic scripts and known error information are valuable at this stage.
Escalation	If the Service Desk cannot handle the incident, *escalation* may be required for additional support. *Functional escalation* involves transferring an incident, problem, or change to a technical team with a higher level of expertise to assist in the escalation. *Hierarchical escalation* is the involvement of senior levels of management to assist in the escalation.
Investigation and diagnosis	If no solution exists yet, the incident is investigated further.
Resolution and recovery	The solution is found and the incident is resolved.
Incident closure	The incident is closed. The Service Desk should check to see that the incident is resolved, and that the user is pleased with the solution.

Problem

Definition:

A *problem* is a root cause of one or more incidents. Details of a problem are documented in a problem record, which contains the entire history of the problem, from discovery to resolution. At the time a problem record is created, it is rare for the cause to be known. For a cloud supplier, the root cause may lie within the services that they provide which may not be compatible to the user's system and may arise as a problem.

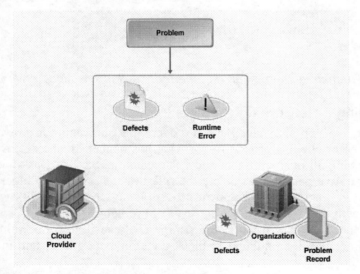

Figure 6-38: A problem is the root cause of incidents.

Example: A Networking Problem

Joseph, an analyst for Ristell & Sons Publishing, finds that he is not leasing an IP address to gain access to the Internet. This disruptive incident prevents him from doing anything, including the use of the company's database to submit a help request. The underlying cause of this incident is a problem. In this case, after some investigation, the IT staff determines that the Ethernet cable connecting the Dynamic Host Configuration Protocol (DHCP) server to the company network had a crimp in it that shorted the signal.

Problem Management

Definition:

Problem Management is a process that attempts to prevent incidents from happening by troubleshooting the root causes of incidents, known in ITIL as problems. Problem Management does not stop at the restoration of the IT service; its ultimate goal is the removal of the underlying cause of the problem. Effective problem management is to discover the root cause of an incident, or series of incidents, and to take appropriate actions to eliminate the root cause. The cloud supplier will have their own priority and time line to eliminate the root cause. The key factor to problem management here is that the role concerning problem management is clearly specified in any contracts or agreements between the cloud supplier and the IT service.

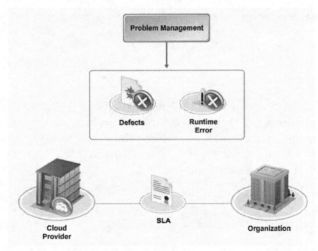

Figure 6-39: Problem management analyzing the root causes in a cloud environment.

Example: Managing a Networking Problem

Carey logs on to her desktop after lunch and discovers that she cannot access any of the company intranet sites. After clicking around to see what has happened, she discovers that her firewall is now blocking all of the intranet sites. She calls the Service Desk and has someone with proper administrative permissions delete the rule in her firewall that blocks all of the internal sites. While the Incident Management process is not concerned with why the error occurred, but only with the restoration of the service, Problem Management wants to know why the error happened, and it will work to learn the root cause. In this case, the cause was a faulty rule that was created in an attempt to block a certain subdomain, but, in fact, the entire domain was blocked.

Activities of Problem Management

The Problem Management process has a number of major activities.

Activity	Description
Detect and log	The problem is detected, or someone has reported it. The problem record is also created.
Categorize and prioritize	The problem is given a type, status, impact, urgency, priority, etc. It is also assigned a prioritization code to manage how it gets handled by staff.
Investigate and diagnose	Determining the root cause of the incident.
Workarounds	Determining a way of getting the service restored while resolving an incident or a problem.
Raise known error	Creating a known error database article that describes the root cause and a work-around.
Problem resolution	A resolution occurs once the problem is permanently fixed, or a work-around is sufficient.
Problem closure	Closure of the problem record.

Request Fulfilment

Definition:

Request Fulfilment is the process responsible for managing the lifecycle of all service requests. It enables users to request and receive standard services, many of which can be given at little to no risk to the organization. Request Fulfilment can also be used to provide information to users and customers about services. Many requests can be logged automatically through a phone menu or an application that allows the user to select specific services themselves in drop-down menus. The process should include appropriate approval before fulfiling the request. It is critical for cloud suppliers to have strict considerations of what can be requested of them and a predefined approval and qualification process will ensure that they are capable of performing the requests submitted to them. All these considerations should be strictly adhered to by the contractual agreements for the benefit of cloud suppliers and users.

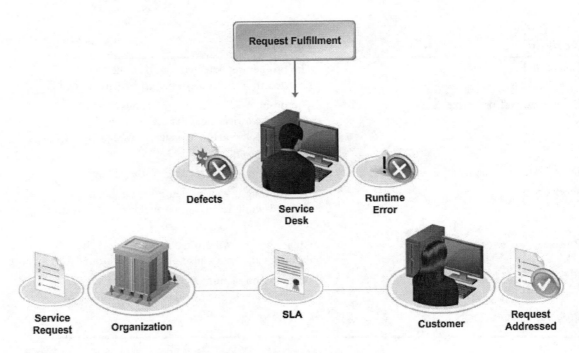

Figure 6-40: *Request fulfilment process in an organization.*

Example: A Typical Request for Fulfilment

Jamie is a Media Developer for Hexa Web Services. She has been assigned to a new project, which requires the use of a software application that is not installed on her computer. She contacts the Service Desk and requests to have a licensed copy of the application placed on her machine.

 Request Fulfilment is new to ITIL v3. Prior to ITIL v3, the process of Request Fulfilment was included in Incident Management.

Activities of Request Fulfilment

The Request Fulfilment process consists of four activities.

Activity	Description
Menu selection	Users place their own requests using service management tools (where applicable), or send a service request to the Service Desk.
Financial authorization	Since most service requests have financial considerations, the cost of fulfiling the request needs to be calculated. In some cases, the prices can be fixed, and the authorization is given instantly. In all other cases, the costs must be estimated and the user must give permission afterwards.
Fulfilment	This activity depends on the actual nature of the request. If it is a simple request, the Service Desk may be able to handle it. If it is more complex, the request is forwarded to a more specialized group.

Activity	Description
Closure	The Service Desk closes the request once the service request has been fulfiled.

Access Management

Definition:

Access Management is the process that grants the right to use an IT service while preventing access to the non-authorized users. Some organizations refer to it as "rights management" or "identity management," but it amounts to the same thing: authorizing and revoking users as they try to use an IT service. One of the great challenges for cloud computing is how secure the cloud can be and it is vital to involve the customer management in the vigilance and planning of access management. All access to cloud services must be monitored and carefully assessed by the clients ITSM organization. An international certification like the *ISO/IEC 27000-series* or others is useful to provide complete assurance in verifying the necessary steps taken to secure cloud access management.

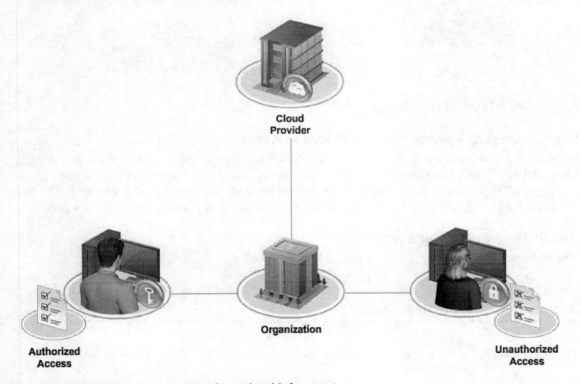

Figure 6-41: *Access management in a cloud infrastructure.*

Example: Changing Access

George is a Network Administrator for eQuiry. After their summer internship program ended, a number of interns were offered full-time jobs for the fall. An official request has come from the human resources department that seven people be converted from intern to employee. Since they had restricted access as interns, they now need to have full access. This includes access to networked drives, access to certain software programs on an application server, write permissions on shared documents, and so on. George is now in charge of granting access rights to these seven new employees.

Rights

Rights are the permissions that users or roles have in relation to an IT service. Rights can also be called privileges. Rights are a fundamental concept in Access Management concerning many different kinds of security, whether physical security, network security, application security, and so on.

Event Management

Definition:

Event Management is a process to monitor events and taking corrective actions to resolve and prevent them. An *event* is an occurrence of an incident indicating that something is not functioning properly and an alert being raised. Some Event Management is automated, which is particularly helpful with software errors that get logged and escalated behind the scenes and without human supervision. In cloud computing, it is substantial to identify all possible alerts and their corrective actions for each cloud supplier. The cloud suppliers should predefine the appropriate actions they would institute to resolve and remove alerts. This will expedite resolving alerts and improve customer satisfaction, and negate unplanned costs ensuring that cloud suppliers do not perform unauthorized actions.

Figure 6-42: Automatic notification of events.

Example: Event Management of Database Access

Michael is a Database Administrator for eQuiry. Joyce, a user who has logged on to a database, had two failed logon attempts before gaining access. As the administrator of that database, Michael is emailed a copy of the logfile showing the failed logon attempts. The notification of this event is automated, and in this case, requires no action on Michael's part.

Activities of Event Management

There are several main activities of Event Management.

Activity	Description
An event occurs	Not all events need to be detected.
Event notification	Events are usually communicated (from a CI, say) in one of two ways: • Polling, which probes for specific data. • A report is created if and only if certain conditions are met.
Event detection	The event is detected by an agent running on the same system, or is transmitted directly to a management tool. The meaning of the event is interpreted. The usage of automation helps to increase the efficiency of event detection and interpretation.

Activity	Description
Event filtering	This is where it is decided whether or not the event should make it to a management tool. Most monitoring tools provide more information than you need; it is important to be able to weigh information properly.
Event classification	The importance of the event is determined. Each business likely has its own way of classifying an event.
Event correlation	This is where the significance of an event is established.
Trigger	If the event is important and significant enough, a response is required. The initiator of the response is called a trigger.
Response options	There are a number of responses that are valid: ● Log the event. ● Allow an automated response to react. ● Create an alert and wait for human intervention. ● Submit a request for change (RFC). ● Open an incident report. ● Open a link to a problem record.
Review actions	This is where you check to see whether an event has been responded to correctly or effectively.
Closing the event	Not all events are closed; some remain open until other actions have been taken.

Technical Management

Definition:

Technical Management is a function within the Service Operation Lifecycle phase that is responsible for providing technical skills for both the general IT infrastructure and for IT service support. Technical Management ensures that all resources required for technical support are trained and deployed to design, build, transition, operate, and improve infrastructure technology. It is critical that technical management is mandatory in all the phases when selecting or employing a cloud service.

Example: Typical Technical Management in the Workplace

Chad is an administrator for Rudison Financial, a large financial services company with a diverse employee base that is geographically spread over the entire world. He is part of the Information Technology Services department, which handles the IT infrastructure of both internal and external requests to access the company network. He ensures that the services within the company, such as the hard-wired network within the buildings of the central campus, and that the virtual networks, including the Virtual Private Network (VPN) that remote employees use to access the company intranet, are available and operational.

IT Operations Management

Definition:

IT Operations Management is accountable for performing the day-to-day activities, operational tasks, functions, and processes. This is true even if there are no customers, no incidents logged, no new services, no changes or improvements, or no service requests. In a cloud service, IT operations management specifications must clearly detail who will perform operations actions and contain the work instructions explaining how to perform those actions. It will lead to greater complications if regular IT operations are not performed appropriately, incurring unplanned costs.

Example: IT Operations Management in the Workplace

vLearners, Inc., an online training company, has a number of activities performed every day that are necessary for the company to function properly. For example, the server room temperature is monitored and maintained so that the central processing units (CPUs) are cooled properly, the network is monitored for any suspicious or malicious traffic, someone must switch tapes during the nightly backups, someone must run batch processing jobs, and so on.

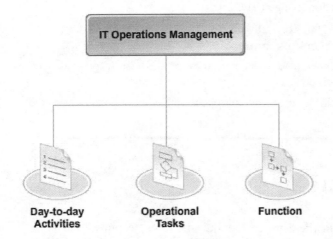

Figure 6-43: Typical IT operations management tasks.

Application Management

Definition:

Application Management is responsible for managing the entire lifecycle of an application. Application Management can also be involved in the design, testing, and improvement of any application that is being used in an IT service. This general, decentralized role is similar to the role that Technical Management plays, with a focus on software applications rather than technological infrastructure. For cloud services, similar to technical management, it is vital that application management be applied to the applications.

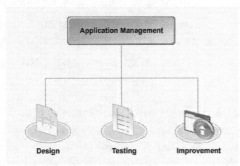

Figure 6-44: *Application Management in an organization.*

Example: Potential Costs and Application Management

Gary is a manager for the Solutions Team at eQuiry, a training company. One of his current projects is to lead a team that is in charge of determining the real costs of a potential application purchase. The choice has come down to purchasing a proprietary program that they would need to then receive paid support for, or else to design and implement a custom application in-house.

Applications vs. Services

It is somewhat common for organizations to refer to applications as services, but it is actually quite a bit more complicated than that. Applications are a component of providing a service, but they are not necessarily synonymous. An application may support more than one service, or a service may make use of many different applications.

How to Mitigate the Risks Involved in Operating Cloud Services

Service Operation encompasses practices for achieving the delivery of agreed levels of services to end-users and customers. To achieve fast and tangible results, it is essential to understand the common risks that pose a potential threat to the delivery of quality services.

Guidelines

- Clear contractual documentation of the service desk roles and responsibilities should be made available to both the cloud users and the cloud providers. If roles and responsibilities are not clearly defined and assigned, it may cause havoc and result in poor customer satisfaction. Also the cloud suppliers will charge extra to provide any services that is undefined in the agreement.

- A synergy should be maintained between the cloud suppliers and the customer's ITSM system to manage the incidents that are disruptive to the delivery of the services.

- Cloud suppliers should be responsible for Incident Lifecycle Ownership to ensure that security breaches do not occur due to excessive workload.

- Cloud suppliers should provide support for the problem management similar to the in-house infrastructure and serve as a crucial point of contact when resolving incidents.

- Cloud suppliers and ITSM customers should be completely engaged in request fulfilment process to ensure that they both agree upon the type of requests submitted to them and manage the cost and service to fulfill the requests.

- Cloud suppliers should have access to the customer's request system to efficiently accept, track, and fulfill requests.

- It is crucial that technology should be employed to identify security breaches and proper action plans are available and applicable to both cloud supplier and consumer ITSM.

- Local infrastructure and cloud technical management should have proper communication channels to meet the requirements of planned or unplanned changes.

- Clear ownership should be defined for cloud operational activities so that the actions can be performed by cloud supplier.

Example: Service Operations in Telecommunication Network Organization

Cindy is a Network Administrator for Hexa Web Services, a large telecommunication network company with a diverse employee base that is geographically spread over the entire world. She is part of the Information Technology Services department, which handles the IT infrastructure of both internal and external requests to access the company network. She makes sure that the services within the company, such as the hard-wired network within the buildings of the central campus, and that the virtual networks, including the Virtual Private Network (VPN) that remote employees use to access the company intranet, are available and operational. To ensure that the services are delivered efficiently, she has defined job roles and responsibility clearly for her department. The service desk responsibilities are clearly documented and knowledge transferred to cloud providers and her department. A clear communication channel is established between the cloud and her organization to resolve incidents and perform problem management efficiently. She also has implemented latest technology to identify security breach, which is both applicable to her organization and to the cloud provider. In addition, she ensured that the cloud provider has complete access to the customer's request system to efficiently accept, track, and fulfill requests.

ACTIVITY 6-5
Understanding the Fundamental Concepts of Service Operation

Scenario:
In this activity, you will discuss the fundamental concepts of the Service Operation phase.

1. **Which of the following is the best example of an incident?**
   a) A DNS Server has had its IP address changed.
   b) A user logs on to her workstation.
   c) A customer attempts to place an order through your company website, and the transaction gets caught in a loop and never completes.
   d) A network drive has reached 65% capacity, which is within the boundaries of the SLA.

2. **Which of the following is the best example of a problem?**
   a) A customer is unable to log on to her account, even after entering her user name and password correctly.
   b) An unauthorized attempt to access the wireless network was blocked.
   c) No one can access a database, and it's discovered that the password database is offline, but the reason for the database to go offline is unknown.

3. **Which of the following occurs in the financial authorization activity of the Request Fulfilment process? Choose all that apply.**
   a) Determining a cost prior to handling the request.
   b) Verifying that the user's budget allows for the request to be made.
   c) Determining the cost after a user makes a request.
   d) Determining that the request falls within your fulfilment budget.

TOPIC F

Continual Service Improvement with Cloud

One of the key phases of the Lifecycle is Continual Service Improvement (CSI), because it encompasses all the other phases; despite any success, you are never finished improving your organization's approach to IT Service Management. In this topic, you will learn how Continual Service Improvement fits into the lifecycle, and how it can be applied to all other lifecycle phases.

Regardless of your organization's success with its service delivery, there can always be improvements in the effectiveness and efficiency of your services and service management processes. By keeping a watchful eye on your own processes, you can be ready to create a value by improving the cost or delivery of any service. A thorough understanding of the Continual Service Improvement (CSI) phase will put you well on your way towards the goal.

Service Reporting

Service Reporting allows you to produce flexible reports that meet the specific business requirements of the organization. For cloud services, it is essential to gather data about the performance from the ongoing activities and develop action plans to improve service and avoid known performance issues.

Action Plans | Cloud Provider | Reports | Organization | Business Requirements

Figure 6-45: *Service reporting producing flexible reports in a cloud infrastructure.*

Service Measurement

The *Service Measurement* process allows you to validate all business decisions that were previously made, direct activities to meet the target, justify the course of action required with an appropriate proof, and intervene to take corrective action. For cloud suppliers, the *Service Measurement Framework* must be established to gather all relevant data and validate and integrate them to deliver services of acceptable service level and look for continual improvements for delivery of quality service.

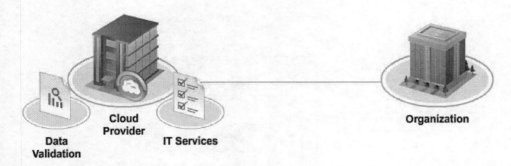

Figure 6-46: Service measurement validating all business decisions in a cloud infrastructure.

Types of Metrics

A metric is a measurement of whether a variable has met its defined goal. There are three types of metrics that support the CSI activities as well as other process activities.

Metric	What it Measures
Technology	Relates to component and application based metrics such as performance and availability.
Process	Relates to *Critical Success Factors (CSFs), Key Performance Indicators (KPIs)* and activity metrics.
Service	Relates to the outcome of the end-to-end service. Component/technology metrics are used to compute the service metrics.

The CSI Model

Continual service improvement is driven by the CSI Model, which is a generic model for the improvement of just about anything. Like the *PDCA Model*, this process is continual, and loops to the beginning once it has finished.

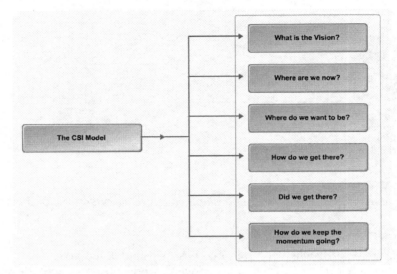

Figure 6-47: The CSI Model for an organization.

Step	Description
What is the vision?	This is where you formulate a vision, define the mission, create goals, and make objectives that work together with the business. This must account for the vision and goals of the customer as well.
Where are we now?	This is where you record a baseline. What is the current level of performance?
Where do we want to be?	This is where you choose measurable, achievable targets. How do you want to measure your target level of improvement?
How do we get there?	This is where you create a detailed Service Improvement Plan (SIP), an outline of specific steps to take to improve the service.
Did we get there?	This is where you see if the objectives have been met, and whether the processes have been complied. This step is measurable and objective.
How do we keep the momentum going?	This is where any change worth keeping is absorbed to be maintained.

Seven Steps of the CSI Process

The CSI process describes how you should actually measure a service and report on your findings.

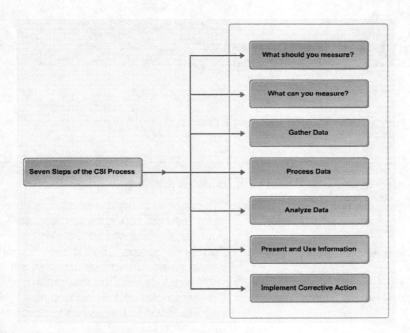

Figure 6-48: Seven steps of the CSI process.

Step	Description
What should you measure?	This follows Phase I of the CSI Model (What is the vision?), and it precedes the assessment of the current state. As with the CSI Model, this must also account for the vision and goals of the customer.
What can you measure?	This step follows Phase V of the CSI Model (Did we get there?). This is about what you are actually capable of measuring. Service providers should reconcile what they should measure and what they can measure.
Gather data	In this step, collect the measurements regarding the organization's vision, mission, goals, and objectives.
Process data	This step prepares relevant data as appropriate; it differs for each audience.
Analyze data	In this step, preparation for the presentation to the business, any trends are extrapolated and possible explanations are gleaned.
Present and use information	At this stage, any stakeholders are informed about whether or not goals have been achieved. This is accomplished objectively with measurements.
Implement corrective action	Relevant improvements are made, a new baseline is established, and the cycle begins again.

ACTIVITY 6-6
Discussing CSI Principles

Scenario:

In this activity, you will discuss the basic CSI principles.

1. **Match the step in the CSI Model with its definition.**

   ___ What is the vision?

   ___ Where are we now?

   ___ Where do we want to be?

   ___ How do we get there?

   ___ Did we get there?

   ___ How do we keep the momentum going?

   a. Choose measurable, achievable targets. How do you want to measure your target level of improvement?

   b. Formulate a vision, define the mission, create goals, and make objectives that work together with the business.

   c. Create a detailed SIP, an outline of specific steps to be taken to improve the service.

   d. Record a baseline. What is the current level of performance?

   e. Any change worth keeping is absorbed to be maintained.

   f. See if the objectives have been met, and whether the processes have been complied. This step is measurable and objective.

2. **During which step of the CSI Process Model are stakeholders informed about whether or not goals have been achieved?**

   a) Process data

   b) Present and use information

   c) Implement corrective action

   d) Analyze data

Lesson 6 Follow-up

In this lesson, you have identified the basic concepts of ITIL, and the phases of the IT Service Management Lifecycle. You also determined how cloud services are resourceful with the implementation of ITIL standards in the organization.

1. **While you might not have used ITIL's exact terminology for the Lifecycle phases in your organization, which Lifecycle phase are you most familiar with?**

2. **What are some IT service practices integrated with cloud computing that exist in your workplace, and where did they come from?**

7 | Identifying Risks and Consequences

Lesson Time: 2 hour(s)

Lesson Objectives:

In this lesson, you will identify the possible risks involved in cloud computing and the risk mitigation measures, and you will also identify the potential cost considerations for the implementation of cloud and its strategic benefits.

You will:

- Identify the organizational risks involved in deploying cloud computing.
- Identify the technical risks involved in deploying cloud computing.
- Identify the legal risks involved in deploying cloud computing.
- Identify and analyze various IT cost factors that influence cloud computing services.
- Identify the mitigation strategies to eliminate the risk factors of cloud computing.

Introduction

Organizations today face challenges not only to develop cost-effective secure IT systems but also other aspects of cloud computing including security and risk. If cloud is not secured properly in their organization, they are concerned with the risks of loss of direct control over systems for which they are nonetheless accountable. In this lesson, you will identify potential risks and learn strategic approaches to manage them. You will also understand the cost considerations for the adoption of cloud computing in an organization.

Every industry comes with its varied levels of risks. For instance, organizations offering financial services need to follow certain data practices, and organizations undertaking software development face risks associated with timely delivery of the product in the market. Therefore, a company deploying cloud computing needs to be aware of the kinds of risks it is likely to face and the ways to tackle them.

TOPIC A
Organizational Risks

Cloud computing poses an additional level of risk because essential services are often outsourced to a third party. The "external" aspect of outsourcing makes it difficult to ensure data integrity and privacy, support data and service availability, and demonstrate compliance. In this topic, you will identify various types of security risks that are involved with cloud computing.

Cloud computing offering a host of benefits has emerged as a promising alternative to the traditional approach to data management. However, it is not without its share of problems because data in cloud can be accessed almost from anywhere, anytime. Understanding the security risks within the application and business environment is, therefore, important because these issues may have a detrimental business impact.

Risk Analysis

Identifying the potential risks to an organization begins with risk analysis. During a risk analysis, the organization determines where there are potential vulnerabilities to specific risks or threats, and analyzes the potential financial loss that would result from these threats.

Figure 7-1: *Risk analysis to check the potential threats in an organization.*

Risk Management

Risk management involves having processes in place to monitor risks, gaining access to reliable and up-to-date information about risks, exercising control when dealing with those risks, and deploying decision-making processes supported by a framework of risk analysis and evaluation. Risk management also involves the identification, selection, and adoption of countermeasures in a way that is most appropriate to the identified risks.

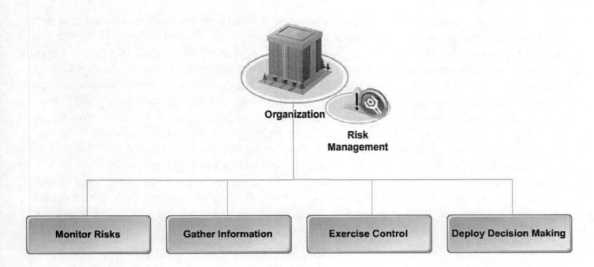

Figure 7-2: Risk management with various functional activities.

Organizational Risks

Cloud security forms an integral part of an organization, and high priority is given to testing and monitoring of security threats to the cloud infrastructure, people and information. Several security challenges arise when cloud services are deployed in an organization. They include:

● The inability on the part of the organization to validate whether a cloud provider is effective in mitigating risks. This is because testing the cloud provider's security measures is hard to arrange and conduct, and the cloud provider may not often agree to it.

● Difficulty knowing where data is stored.

● Difficulty retrieving, or removing the data or code in a cloud service provider's system.

● Technical failures that could destroy the stored data.

● Issues around data retrieval if a cloud provider goes out of business, and

● Unauthorized access of data by others.

Figure 7-3: Organizational risks with cloud services deployed in an organization.

Vendor Lock-In

Consumers may face many challenges that arise concerning data, application and service portability issues once they have entered into a service agreement with a cloud provider, also known as vendor lock-in. Once a service agreement is in place with a cloud provider, changing that decision can prove to be challenging; migrating data and services back to an in-house IT environment or choosing another cloud provider can be costly and time consuming. Consumers are dependent on the cloud provider, and put their business and important data at risk if the cloud provider is unable to meet their requirements on schedule or if the provider ever stops providing the cloud services. SaaS cloud providers create custom specific applications to suit the client's requirements, and any change will incur extra financial charges to the cloud consumers. Therefore, it is essential to evaluate all the aspects in the legal agreement before migration of data to cloud services. With PaaS, APIs can vary for each cloud provider, resulting in compatibility issue for cloud consumers. With IaaS, data storage varies between cloud providers, and application level dependence, such as access controls, may limit the consumer's choices when selecting a provider.

Data Storage

Service Provider

Organization

Figure 7-4: Vendor lock-in with data portability issue in an organization.

Loss of Management Control

When IT services employ third-party cloud services, cloud providers take control of all the data and applications which in turn may affect cloud consumers. In addition, SLAs may not comply with consumer requirements and render any commitment from the cloud provider invalid, thus widening the security coverage gap. Cloud providers may employ third-party vendors to complete service deliverables and this may in turn lead to change in control of the cloud providers, resulting in security breaches and new terms and conditions. Data integrity, loss of governance and control, performance deterioration of quality services, lack of confidentiality, and security breaches contribute to a very high risk factor for IaaS providers. It is comparatively low for SaaS providers.

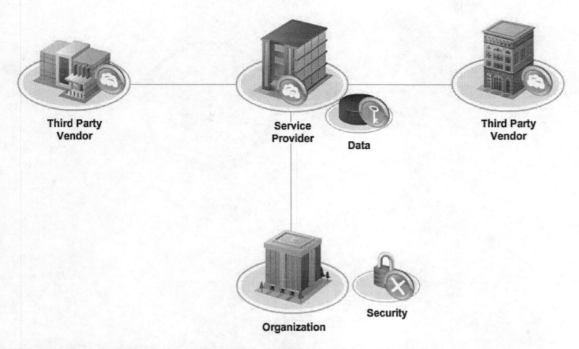

Figure 7-5: *Loss of governance leading to security gap in an organization.*

National Vulnerability Database (NVD) and Common Weaknesses Enumeration (CWE)

Web application scanners should be up to date with the vulnerabilities and attack paths mentioned in the *National Vulnerability Database (NVD)* and *Common Weaknesses Enumeration (CWE)*. Firewalls specific to web applications should be installed to mitigate the existing vulnerabilities. The NVD is a government based repository of standards consisting of security checklists, security related software flaws, misconfigurations, product names, and impact metrics.

CWE is now maintained by the MITRE Corporation with support from the National Cyber Security Division. CWE represents a single vulnerability type such as *input validation, information leak/disclosure, cross-site scripting (XSS), authentication issues* and many more.

Compliance with Regulations

It is essential that cloud providers offer assurance to the cloud consumer via audit certification. Cloud providers may fail to provide certification to consumers, or the certification schemes adopted by them may not comply with consumer requirements. For example, cloud providers may opt to use open source hypervisors or custom versions which do not comply with fundamental objectives of government public sectors. The location of data is unclear, and redundant data storage without adequate information on jurisdiction of storage amounts to violating the regulations. The risk level is very high for each delivery model of cloud service.

Figure 7-6: Compliance regulations at an organizational level.

Lack of Resources

When cloud services are deployed, and there are more than one tenants involved in sharing cloud resources, data privacy is compromised, resulting in loss of sensitive or confidential information. Resource allocation of one tenant can affect another co-tenant as it becomes easy for them to map another customer's data to a virtual hard drive and copy or retrieve confidential information. This may also lead to disastrous results as it allows an outsider to easily manipulate the vulnerabilities inside the cloud facility. Cloud providers risk the loss of business reputation because of illegal data access by co-tenants and poor quality of service. The risk level is medium for each delivery model of cloud service.

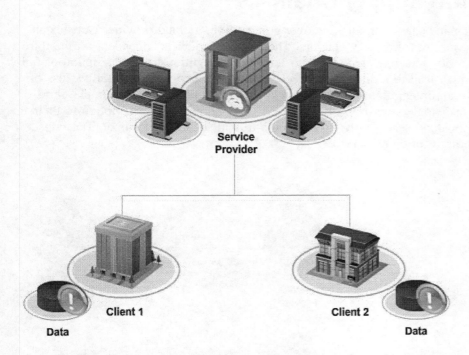

Figure 7-7: *Lack of resources leading to illegal access of data in a cloud infrastructure.*

Failure of Cloud Service

A cloud service may succumb to a new technology, competitive pressure, an inadequate business strategy, or lack of financial support, and run out of business or restructure the service offerings being provided to cloud consumers. This leads to failure or termination of cloud services. Cloud consumers fail to meet the commitments to their own customers. Moreover, they are exposed to the contractual liability with cloud providers. The impact and risk level is medium for the IaaS, SaaS and PaaS delivery models of cloud services.

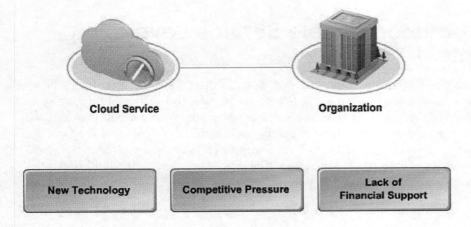

Figure 7-8: *Failure of cloud services due to various critical factors.*

Failure of the Supply Chain

To meet growing demands and gain an edge over competition, a cloud provider can subcontract specialized services to third-party vendors. The cloud provider is dependent on the third party for overall security and may abide by their terms and conditions. Any disruption or failure in their service may lead to a disastrous effect resulting in service unavailability, loss of data confidentiality, data integration, and violation of contractual terms. For example, third-party vendors may use single sign-on or identity management, and any interruption to their services or cloud providers' services may weaken the trust of a cloud consumer. The impact and risk level is medium for cloud services.

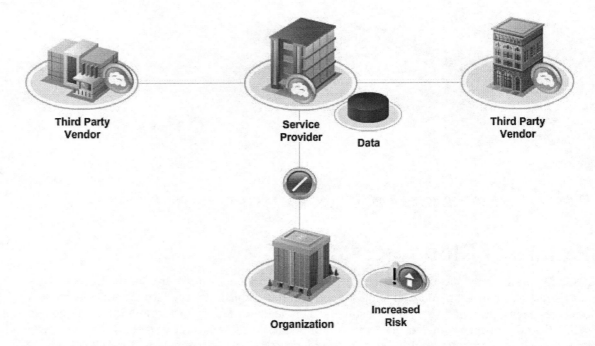

Figure 7-9: *Failure of the supply chain in an organization.*

Incorrect or Incompatible Service Level Agreements

Service Level Agreements are legal contracts used to settle disputes over the delivery of service. Cloud providers and cloud consumers define SLAs to establish responsibility for specific activities and to identify the potential risks for services. Acquisition of a cloud provider will result in non-binding agreements, and SLAs vary for each cloud consumer and may not comply with their security requirements. This will adversely affect a company's reputation, and its customers and employees within the organization. The risk level, though medium for each cloud delivery model, cannot be ignored.

Figure 7-10: Incompatible Service Level Agreements with disastrous effects in an organization.

ACTIVITY 7-1

Understanding the Security Risks Associated with Cloud Computing

Scenario:

In this activity, you will review your knowledge of the security risks associated with the adoption of cloud.

1. **What happens to cloud providers when they face a new market technology, competitive pressure, an inadequate business strategy, or lack of financial support?**

    a) They run out of business, lose their services or restructure their business services.

    b) They look for more financial support.

    c) They allocate new resources.

    d) They cancel the SLAs.

2. **Name the security risk factors associated with the delivery model of cloud services. (Choose Three.)**

    a) Scalability

    b) Loss of management control

    c) Lock-in

    d) Compliance regulations

TOPIC B
Technical Risks

You are now familiar with the business risks involved in deploying cloud services. However, it is essential to know the factors that influence resource allocation in cloud, and the risks which delay or hinder the access of data and hardware resources. In this topic, you will identify the technical risks associated with the adoption of cloud services.

Cloud computing is fast emerging as a technology that helps maximize the utilization of resources with minimal cost of investment. Since this technology is exposed to inherent risks, such as improper provisioning of infrastructure, network outages, and security issues, it is essential to resolve such issues and obtain maximum benefits.

Incorrect Provisioning of Resources

The concept of cloud revolves around the fact that hardware and software resources are available to organizations on a shared and on-demand basis. Service providers allocate resources to consumers based on statistical projections. The allocation of resources by service providers to IT organizations is prone to certain disadvantages such as:

- Inadequate investment in provisioning of hardware resources.
- The likelihood of high priority application or server crashes, leading to services being unavailable.
- Distributed Denial of Service attacks (DDoS).
- Under provisioning of resources leading to reduced profits.
- And, compromise of control measures when accessing information and resources due to improper provisioning of resources.

Technical Security Issues

The cloud infrastructure is primarily based on the key feature of multi-tenancy, wherein multiple systems access an instance of the software which runs on a server. In cloud, the computing systems, network, storage, and applications are shared by multiple users. The risks involved in using public cloud services are usually far greater when compared to private cloud services. While public cloud is exposed to usage by many people, the usage of the private cloud is restricted to an organization.

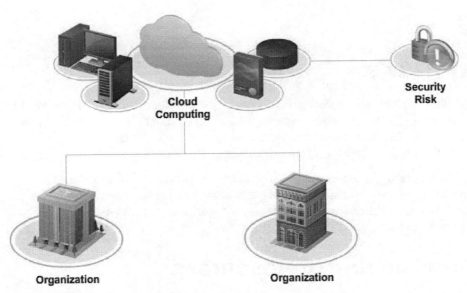

Figure 7-11: *Technical security issues in an organization.*

It is possible that a user may encounter security risks when acquiring cloud services.

Security Issues	Description
Interception of data in transit	When you use cloud computing, more data is likely to be in transit than in cloud data centers, which means data has to be encrypted at all phases to avoid the risk of interception, such as ● Spoofing attack: A spoofing attack is a situation in which one person or program is disguised as a legitimate user by faking data and gaining an illegal advantage. ● Man-in-the-Middle (MitM) attack: A form of eavesdropping in which a person or program makes independent connections with two people communicating with each other and intercepts the messages.
Improper identity management systems	It refers to the lack of a structured identity management system that service providers should maintain to authenticate privileged users.
Data protection	There are many possibilities of data leaks in cloud due to malware and hacking, and as a result the security and integrity of data are highly questionable.
Loss of encryption keys	Disclosure of passwords and secret security keys to outsiders results in the leak of critical and personal data stored in the cloud.

Hypervisor Layer Risks

The hypervisor is known as the virtualization of hardware resources, because multiple operating systems run concurrently on a host machine. When there is an attack on the hypervisor layer, it is possible to intrude and hack the virtualized systems controlled by the hypervisor.

Denial of Service

As an on-demand computing technology, cloud computing and the resources allocated to customers on the cloud face technical risks such as *Economic Denial of Sustainability (EDoS)* and *Distributed Denial of Service (DDoS)* attacks. The DDoS attack is a major threat to the cloud provider as well as the customer. It is an attempt to prevent intended users from utilizing a service hosted on a site. Attackers may pose a threat to cloud vendors by extracting a huge sum of money in exchange for stopping the attacks.

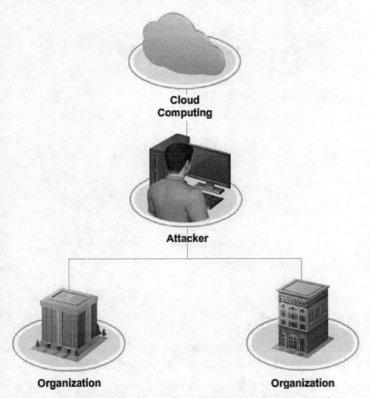

Figure 7-12: *Denial of service attack in an organization.*

An Economic Denial of Sustainability (EDoS) attack, on the other hand, is a technique used by cloud service providers. EDoS aims at making the cloud cost unsustainable, reducing organizations affordability to procure cloud services.

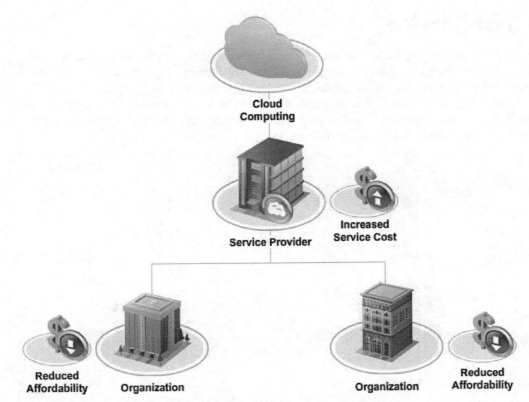

Figure 7-13: *Economic denial of sustainability in an organization.*

Management of IT Resources

In a public cloud, any user can access the resources and applications via the Internet. There are many issues around the management of resources in cloud computing. The issues include:

● Network connectivity – Since cloud computing operates on a wide network of infrastructure, it is exposed to the risk of handling heavy load, resulting in low performance levels, unsecured application management, and high latency levels.

● Service contract – The security assurance given in the SLA by the service provider may be insufficient and not defined clearly, resulting in data loss and jurisdiction issues.

● Authentication mechanism – Uncontrolled identity management principles applied by providers result in unprivileged users accessing data.

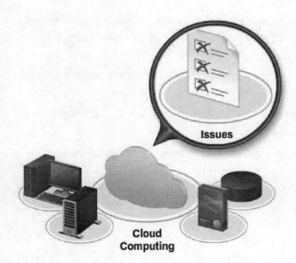

Figure 7-14: *Management of IT resources in an organization.*

Risk of the Service Engine

The service engine is a software component that runs on the hardware resources at the service provider's location. It helps organizations access the applications and utilize the resources in cloud computing. The service engine is prone to these risks:

The service engine is a software component modeled above hardware resources in the service provider's location. It helps organizations access the applications and utilize the resources in cloud. The service engine is prone to these risks:

- Unauthorized access to the pool of applications in the cloud (SaaS cloud).

- Modification of data without direct intervention on the application in the customer environment (PaaS cloud).

- Hacking of virtual machines in the cloud using malware, resulting in fewer resources being assigned and causing denial of service (IaaS cloud).

Network Outages

A network outage is a major risk factor associated with a public cloud, as it results in more system downtime, and data loss in web application portals. Contractual agreements delivered to customers are often non-negotiable. In case of network outages, providers give minimal or no guarantee against data loss including catastrophic loss. Also, during an outage, traffic diversion to any other data center is minimal as there is no proper coordination between service providers.

Physical Security Risks

It is imperative that the SLA clearly segregates responsibilities between service providers and consumers to ensure the physical security of the infrastructure. Some of the risk factors to physical security are:

● Malicious users – Malicious users may compromise the security measures adopted by service providers.

● Effect of performance risks – In a multi-tenant environment, heavy usage of resources by one user will impact the quality of service rendered to other users.

● Cross network traffic listening – Hackers may misuse data when proper patches are not applied on host machines.

● Theft of equipment – Poor security measures adopted by providers may result in any outsider trespassing and stealing physical resources.

ACTIVITY 7-2
Identifying the Technical Risks Associated with Cloud Computing

Scenario:

In this activity, you will review your knowledge about the technical risks associated with the adoption of cloud computing.

---

1. **True or False? In a public cloud, service providers give complete assurance for data security.**

   ___ True

   ___ False

---

2. **When does an organization become prone to a man-in-the-middle attack?**

   a) When there is a denial of service.

   b) When there is a loss of encryption keys.

   c) When there is interception of data in transit.

TOPIC C
Legal Risks

You are aware of technical risks associated with the adoption of cloud computing services. It is essential to know the various legal risk factors which contribute to data loss and customer dissatisfaction. In this topic, you will identify the legal risks that contribute to unfavorable conditions for adopting cloud computing services.

Organizations should analyze the risk factors linked with obtaining cloud services. An organization using cloud services may face IT related risks, such as unwanted data disclosure, change in jurisdiction, and licensing issues, that are legal in nature. It is essential for you to prepare yourself to manage and mitigate such legal risks to successfully acquire cloud services.

Risks Due to Legislation

Cloud services are widely used in industries such as healthcare, telecommunication, financial, and banking. The availability of data in the cloud is subject to several legal risks.

Risk Factors	Description
Jurisdiction issues	Since interoperability is the key component of cloud services, data is stored in multiple jurisdictions, resulting in lack of transparency. Consider the case of data being stored in countries where enforcement laws don't comply with international agreements. In such cases, data is exposed to the risk of enforced disclosure and seizure. When different jurisdictions apply their own rules, the situation becomes complex because the risk of data being disclosed becomes much greater.
New data streams	Cloud computing is basically modeled to store large collections of data pertaining to many organizations. The possibility of creating and misusing a new data stream from the data collection in the cloud is much greater.
Data security	The procurement of cloud services is not hindered by the geographic location, and so data security is a major concern. The main risks to data security in the cloud include: • Inadequate measures adopted to ensure data security • Loss of data by service providers • Unauthorized access to data • Hackers or viruses targeting service providers, resulting in the loss of, or damage to data and resources in the cloud
Lawful access	When multiple organizations use the services of centralized management systems like within the cloud, a request for lawful access of and acquiring information is very vital, to avoid access to information beyond the scope of lawful access legislation.
Data processing	Organizations adopting cloud services should ensure that service providers ensure data security at all times. In addition, the process for access to, and correction and deletion of procedures should be robust and foolproof.

Risk Factors	Description
Data permanence	Organizations enter into contractual agreements with service providers to store data, and use the applications in the cloud. It is vital that consumers consider the security of data after the contract expiry. Standards should be implemented to ensure that copies of data are not stored in the cloud even after contractual agreement expiration.

Data Protection Laws

Laws that enforce data security and protection abound in cloud computing, and cloud providers should ensure that they abide by these laws.

Data Protection Norms	Descriptions
Through Supervision of the SLA and contractual agreements	Organizations should scrutinize the terms and conditions mentioned by service providers in contractual agreements and SLAs to interpret the guarantee they provide for securing data in the cloud.
Swiss Data Protection Law	• The law enforces that the data controller alone is responsible for data security even though data is processed by any other vendor or a third party. • The transfer of personal data to storage locations in different countries is allowed only if data protection is in accordance to Swiss Standards. • Adoption of technical measures and standards to maintain confidentiality, integrity and availability of data should be implemented.
Data Protection Act 1998	The law states that data can be stored in any country outside Europe, but the business is ultimately responsible for the data. It is essential to understand the norms of the SLA to identify the level of responsibility the service provider has with respect to data, and ensure data security and that the provisions for compensation following a security breach are available.
Periodical Audit Measures	These pertain to the audit measures adopted by consumers and service providers to ensure data security.

Licensing Risks

One of the major concerns in adopting cloud services is how to control the use of web applications with software licenses. The three main software license types are:

- Per-user – A user is granted a license to use the application in the cloud.
- Per-device – The license is granted based on the total number of processors used to acquire cloud services.
- Enterprise – The license is granted to the organization as a whole, regardless of the number of users accessing the applications in the cloud.

There are a few risks associated with the licensing of resources in the cloud.

- Service providers dynamically provision the servers in the cloud to meet the increase in demand and improve performance levels, reduce latency, and optimize load balancing. The major concern is to provide an appropriate license in such a situation.

- Online licensing checks may not be applicable for cloud services because if the use of a software application is charged per instance of use, the customer is at risk of incurring a high cost regardless of the number of machine instances for the same duration.

- In the case of PaaS and SaaS computing services, where the development and utilization of web applications are the major tasks involved, it is essential to abide by appropriate clauses in the contracts with service providers to eliminate the risk of violating license agreements.

ACTIVITY 7-3
Identifying the Legal Risks Associated with Cloud Computing

Scenario:

In this activity, you will review your knowledge on the legal risk factors dominant in the cloud computing environment.

1. **What are the legislation risks involved while adopting cloud services? (Choose all that apply.)**

   a) Data permanence

   b) Jurisdiction issues

   c) High cost and latency

   d) Lawful access

2. **True or False? Online licensing checks help ensure the availability of software licenses when adopting cloud services.**

   ___ True

   ___ False

TOPIC D
Cost Evaluation for Cloud Computing

Cloud computing simplifies an organization's existing systems and infrastructure, by enabling their business to maintain IT infrastructure more efficiently. Success is achieved by consolidation of IT resources resulting in the reduction of cost of running and managing IT – thereby enhancing business performance for a sound return on investment. In this topic, you will identify various cost factors that influence cloud computing services.

The cost benefits of implementing cloud services vary depending upon the size of the organization and its existing IT resources/overheads including data center infrastructure, hardware, software, IT staffing and technical skill resource. Understanding the strategic costs and benefits supports a rational economic approach to cloud adoption.

Direct Cost vs. Indirect Cost

Definition:

When determining the provisioning value of a service, it may be tricky to determine the actual cost. A *direct cost* is a cost that can be allocated to a specific service for a customer. Any cost that can be directly tied to providing one specific service for a client would be a direct cost. An *indirect cost* is one that is used to support multiple services, or a service that is provided to multiple groups of customers. The precise benefit of one specific service is difficult or sometimes even impossible to compute. Examples of indirect costs might include a company's telephone usage or electricity bill.

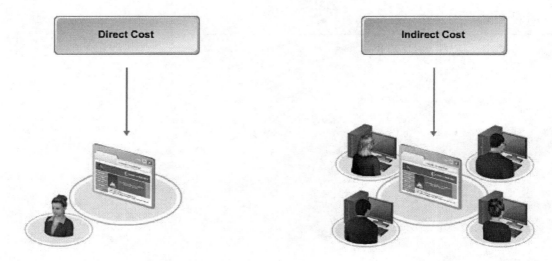

Figure 7-15: Direct vs. indirect costs in an organization.

Example: A Direct and Indirect Cost

Rudison Technologies is attempting to calculate the costs of providing a service for a specific client. The company had to purchase a server that is dedicated to running email software for just this client. This is logged as a direct cost, as the individual service and client are very clear. However, the company has recently renewed its facility contract to be able to house all of its servers in operation, including the one just purchased. This is an indirect cost, as it supports more than just a single service.

Total Cost of Ownership

Definition:

The *Total Cost of Ownership* (TCO) is a cost calculation designed to evaluate direct and indirect costs of a product or system. The objective is to arrive at a final estimation which reflects the total effective costs of all purchases made in an organization. TCO analysis is therefore crucial for organizations who scale their applications, to use and pay only for the resources their applications consume. Some of the general guidelines that provide a useful insight for TCO analysis include.

- **Identify all the cost components that contribute to the TCO analysis in an organization** – For example, a cloud provider may charge for the usage of resources, network traffic and data storage. In addition, the cloud provider may also provide a permanent IP address associated with the application. Consumers are caught unaware for the extra charges that are levied on the user for not using the IP address.

- **Identify and assess the combination of cloud services which are useful to an individual organization** – Some applications involve computing and others are used to process large amounts of data. Understanding the nature of your application to assign costs to the different cloud services enables you to obtain a clear picture of TCO.

- **Identify and understand the role of capacity in an application** – If the capacity for your application varies significantly, it adversely affects all other resources. It is important to evaluate your TCO for a number of application topologies to understand the costs for various capacity levels.

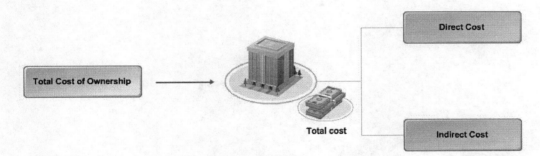

Figure 7-16: *Total cost of ownership with sub cost components.*

Example: TCO for Hexa Constructions Company

Hexa Constructions needed to scale its operations in multiple divisions located throughout the state. To do a complete TCO analysis, they decided to evaluate the direct and indirect costs that are incurred by the organization in each division. They found that licensed software, licensed software support services and professional services were the important cost factors. The TCO model was further refined to include other current project costs estimates.

Impact of Indirect Costs on TCO

While indirect costs are intangible in nature, and difficult to measure, they definitely cause an impact on TCO. Some of the indirect cost factors that affect TCO include:

- Reliability and availability: When there are failed interactions, it results in the loss of time and loss of business opportunities. In this case, users are persuaded to try the technology with more resistance. More emphasis is provided as to what SLAs are offered by the cloud vendors and how do they comply with the internal staff of an organization?

- Interoperability: Is it easy for cloud services to integrate with other applications?

- Extensibility: Can a cloud vendor customize solutions easily to fit the needs of an organization?

- Security: It can lead to a security breach if sensitive or confidential information is shared outside the cloud infrastructure. What are the security policies that are in place with a cloud provider and how do they comply with the internal policies?

- Scalability: As the business grows, the infrastructure should be able to meet the increasing demands. Can a cloud provider accommodate growth and what are the costs associated with internal applications?

- Capacity: To determine the usage and adoption level within an enterprise is tedious. With SaaS cloud services, these are easily managed.

- Opportunity costs: Non availability of IT resources/overheads including data center infrastructure and IT staffing and technical skill resources causes a delay in the production. These costs have a direct impact on the company.

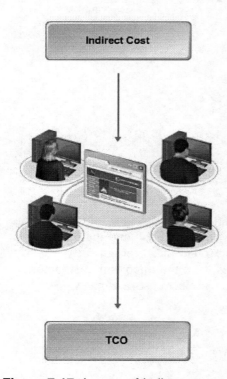

Figure 7-17: Impact of indirect costs on TCO in an organization.

TCO for SaaS, PaaS and IaaS

In the case of cloud computing, many organizations find it difficult to assess the total costs of cloud-based applications because the amount of resources differs for each delivery model of cloud service.

Cloud Delivery Model	Total Cost of Ownership
SaaS	For a SaaS cloud provider, there are no software licenses to buy. They have a recurring cost structure, which includes an annual or monthly subscription fee for the cloud services you use.
	It is easy to deploy SaaS applications for lesser costs in comparison to traditional software solutions, avoiding the hidden costs in deploying, running and maintaining the traditional software. For SaaS vendors, it is difficult to customize the applications to fit the business process.
PaaS	For a PaaS cloud provider, they do not invest in buying systems, software, platforms, and resources to build, run and deploy the application and therefore TCO is low for them.
	They follow the cloud service model – pay per use model. The TCO analysis for PaaS applications depends on the number of users inclusive of software developers, testers, or business users. Sometimes, it may prove to be more expensive than an on-premise solution.
IaaS	For IaaS cloud providers, you can outsource your IT infrastructure and save costs. IaaS offers a low TCO in comparison to traditional IT infrastructure. There are no server maintenance costs, no ongoing IT support costs or operation cost involved.
	All help desk, maintenance and server administration is covered by the low monthly infrastructure as a service fee.

Return on Investment (ROI)

Return on Investment (ROI) is a performance metric used to measure the efficiency of an investment. To estimate ROI, the net income of an investment is divided by the total cost of an investment; the end result is expressed as a percentage. By analyzing the benefits offered by cloud computing, you can easily calculate the potential returns from a business perspective.

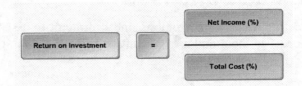

Figure 7-18: ROI calculation.

ROI of Cloud Computing

Some of the cloud computing benefits that contribute towards a profitable ROI are listed.

- Cost Savings: Cloud not only eliminates the need for IT infrastructure / resources and the need to hire additional overheads to manage on-premise solutions. It also facilitates the upgrades and ongoing maintenance of the process.

- Increased Focus: Cloud migration improves service levels across the organization by focusing on Web-access programs, and improving operations.

- Predictability: Service Level agreements are defined between cloud providers and consumers so that cloud providers adhere to specific deliverables at the specified cost or face penalty in case of disruption of services, whereas internal departments are distracted with competing internal projects and unforeseen issues.

- Improved Visibility: Transition to cloud facilitates the use of identity management and improves reporting and visibility into how the solution is being used.

ACTIVITY 7-4

Identifying the Cost Factors Associated with Cloud Computing

Scenario:

In this activity, you will review your knowledge about the cost factors associated with cloud computing services.

1. **Identify the indirect costs that affect TCO in an organization.**

   a) Security.

   b) Value-added services.

   c) Scalability.

   d) Interoperability.

2. **What is the correct definition of TCO?**

   a) TCO provides value added services to a customer.

   b) TCO identifies only the intangible costs associated with a product or system.

   c) TCO is a cost calculation designed to evaluate direct and indirect costs of a product or system.

   d) TCO is a performance metric used to measure the efficiency of an investment.

3. **Identify the various cost factors for an IaaS cloud provider. (Choose all that apply.)**

   a) No server maintenance costs.

   b) No ongoing IT support costs or operation costs involved.

   c) No outsourcing of IT infrastructure.

   d) Low subscription fees for the IT help desk.

TOPIC E
Identify Maintenance Aspects of Strategic Flexibility

You have identified risks and evaluated the cost of transforming operations to cloud. You may now want to know the strategic measures that help you overcome the risks factors and easily move your IT operations to the cloud. In this topic, you will identify the measures for achieving strategic flexibility in the cloud.

Imagine an expensive painting that you think would look perfect in your drawing room. You need to give attention to minor details before purchasing it. Similarly, it is essential to identify the key factors that contribute to the maintenance of strategic flexibility, well before adopting to cloud services. This will help you in evaluating the benefits of transforming your operations to the cloud.

Strategic Flexibility

Strategic flexibility is an approach adopted by an organization to anticipate and prepare themselves for uncertain scenarios in the future. In the cloud, it is essential for organizations to analyze and ascertain the process of transferring operations as cloud migration is not a simple task. It involves a series of incremental steps to ensure that the organization can align its business goals with the cloud technology and infrastructure to sell its product portfolio.

It is essential for organizations to analyze and ascertain the process of transferring operations to cloud computing, because cloud migration is not a simple task. It involves a series of incremental steps to ensure that the organization can align its business goals with the cloud technology and infrastructure to sell its product portfolio.

Factors That Enable Strategic Flexibility

There are multiple factors that can help organizations to obtain strategic flexibility when adopting to cloud services.

Factors	Description
Organizational Demand and Selection of the Appropriate Cloud Model	Organizations can choose the desired cloud model, based on their chief demands and requirements. • Public Cloud – Organizations without clearly defined demand levels can adopt public cloud services as their demand for resources is variable and not constant. • Private Cloud – Organizations with clearly defined and constant demand cycles can opt for private cloud services. • Hybrid Cloud – Organizations aiming to segregate their workload in the correct environments (public and private) can adapt to hybrid cloud services.

Factors	Description
Targeting Economic Benefits	Organizations should investigate the subscription fee schedule of the service provider, as it may not directly reflect the cost of set-up, cost incurred for transitioning the services to the cloud, and cost of data storage and redundancy. Additionally, users must thoroughly scrutinize the SLA for vendor penalties in the event of breach of trust.
Ascertaining the Cost of Adapting Cloud Computing	Organizations should be aware of the cost of transitioning to cloud computing, before choosing the cloud model best suited to their needs. It is vital to know whether the service provider should restructure resources and rewrite applications to cater to organizational requirements. In such a case, the cost of investment will be significant and there is a possibility of vendor lock-in as complete product development of the user is dependent on the cloud service provider.

Factors	Description
Evaluation of the Amortization Value of Existing IT Investments	Before opting to move to cloud computing, organizations should determine the impact of a cloud model on the cost of depreciation of their existing IT investments. With virtualization being the key component of cloud, it is possible to extend the existing security frameworks to the cloud for ensuring data protection.
Rapid Provisioning of Resources	Service providers should be able to provide hardware resources specific to consumer demands and support automation of the process of managing the virtual sprawling of IT resources.
Measuring the Value of Cloud Computing	Organizations should make alterations to the existing strategies, procedures, standards, teams and processes to accommodate the services of cloud. Without implementing the appropriate management disciplines, the adoption of cloud services can lead to security issues, increased cost of operations, and compliance issues.
Need for Cloud and Future Opportunities	Organizations should aim at developing a cloud strategy from a business perspective so that it is compatible with both present and future needs.

Approaches for Maintaining Strategic Flexibility

Organizations adopting cloud computing should also adopt strategic measures to acquire the maximum benefits across their business and not just a specific area.

Measures	Description
Dynamic use of IT resources	This involves centralized procurement and management of IT resources with anticipated cost of operations and acquiring additional resources from service providers to meet high demands of business.
Monitoring the model	This involves following up with cross-cloud integrations to be able to derive reliable usage, and adapting to risk mitigation measures and improved latency levels.
Security	It is essential to evaluate risk factors such as data security, integrity, recovery and backup as they are critical to the adoption of cloud.
Cost Structure	Organizations should ascertain methods to make optimal use of cloud to reduce the capital on investment, and realize faster revenue growth, increased return on assets (ROA) and low operational costs.
Virtualized Infrastructure	Organizations should choose the right storage platform for shared resources to reap the benefits of increased performance levels, and improved business benefits.
Compliance and Governance requirements	Organizations should thoroughly scrutinize the compliance measures adopted by providers such as: • Encryption Standards • Audit • Data location • Physical and environmental control of resources • Identity Management • Scheduled Maintenance plans • Detection and Forensics

ACTIVITY 7-5
Identifying the Steps to Maintain Strategic Flexibility

Scenario:

In this activity, you will review your knowledge of the various factors that aid in maintaining strategic flexibility in cloud.

1. **True or False? Organizations with defined demand levels can adopt public cloud services as their demand for resources is always constant.**

   ___ True

   ___ False

2. **What compliance and governance requirements should be ascertained by organizations before opting for cloud services? (Choose all that apply.)**

   a) Audit

   b) Monitoring the cloud model

   c) Detection and Forensics

   d) Encryption Standards

Lesson 7 Follow-up

In this lesson, you identified the risks involved and the risk mitigation measures in cloud computing. You also were able to identify the various cost factors that are involved with cloud computing. Overcoming risks is the chief concern of any organization. This can be implemented by measuring performance, securing data and applications, and tracking and documenting resources.

1. **What are the risks that you are likely to encounter while implementing cloud computing? Why?**

2. **What kind of mitigation measures do you expect to adopt to ensure the security of your data on the cloud? Discuss.**

Follow-up

In this course, you weighed the pros and cons of cloud computing to make effective decisions in meeting the IT challenges of an organization.

1. **What kinds of cloud services will you use in your organization and why?**

2. **Which do you think is the most critical step in adopting cloud services?**

What's Next?

After completing this course and taking time for additional review of the course materials, you may pursue training and certification in other IT areas such as CompTIA®'s A+®, Network+®, Security+®, or Server+®; (ISC)²®'s Certified Information Services Security Professional (CISSP)®; or ISACA®'s Certified Information Security Manager (CISM)®. You may also want to consider security certifications from other organizations in the IT security field, such as Cisco®, Microsoft®, Juniper®, or SANS™.

Mapping Course Content to the CompTIA® Cloud Essentials™ (Exam CLO-001) Exam Objectives

Exam Objective	Cloud Essentials Certification Lesson and Topic Reference
Domain 1.0 Characteristics of Cloud Services from a Business Perspective	
1.1 Understand common terms and definitions of cloud computing and provide examples.	
1.4 Understand several common definitions of cloud computing and their commonalities/differences.	
● Cloud Computing	Lesson 1, Topic A
● Components of the Cloud	Lesson 1, Topic A
● Clients	Lesson 1, Topic A
● Types of Clients	Lesson 1, Topic A
● Networks	Lesson 1, Topic A
● The Web Application Programming Interface	Lesson 1, Topic A
● Key Characteristics of Cloud Computing	Lesson 1, Topic A
● Types of Cloud	Lesson 1, Topic A
● Cloud Deployment Models	Lesson 1, Topic A
● Advantages of Cloud Computing	Lesson 1, Topic A
● The History of Cloud Computing	Lesson 1, Topic B
● On-Demand Computing Solution Models	Lesson 1, Topic B

Exam Objective	Cloud Essentials Certification Lesson and Topic Reference
1.2 Describe the relationship between cloud computing and virtualization.	
• Cloud Computing vs. Virtualization	Lesson 1, Topic B

Exam Objective	Cloud Essentials Certification Lesson and Topic Reference
1.3 Name early examples of cloud computing.	
• Cloud Computing vs. Grid and Utility Computing	Lesson 1, Topic B
• Cloud Computing vs. the Client-Server Model	Lesson 1, Topic B
• Cloud Computing vs. the Peer-to-Peer Model	Lesson 1, Topic B

Exam Objective	Cloud Essentials Certification Lesson and Topic Reference
1.5 Recognize what types organizations might benefit from cloud computing.	
• Types of Business That Benefit from Cloud	Lesson 2, Topic A

Exam Objective	Cloud Essentials Certification Lesson and Topic Reference
1.6 Recognize what types organizations might not benefit from cloud computing.	
• Types of Business That May Not Benefit from Cloud	Lesson 2, Topic A

Exam Objective	Cloud Essentials Certification Lesson and Topic Reference
1.7 Distinguish between the different types of clouds, including XaaS, IaaS, PaaS, and give examples of them.	
• Types of Cloud	Lesson 1, Topic A
• Distributed Computing as a Service	Lesson 1, Topic C
• Databases as a Service	Lesson 1, Topic C
• Cache as a Service	Lesson 1, Topic C
• Parallelism as a Service	Lesson 1, Topic C
• Sharding	Lesson 1, Topic C
• The Database Profiler	Lesson 1, Topic C

Exam Objective	Cloud Essentials Certification Lesson and Topic Reference
Domain 2.0 Cloud Computing and Business Value	
2.1 Recognize the similarities and differences between cloud computing and outsourcing.	
● On-Demand Computing Solution Models	Lesson 1, Topic B

Exam Objective	Cloud Essentials Certification Lesson and Topic Reference
2.2 Understand the following characteristics of clouds and cloud services from a business perspective: ● *Scalability* ● *Security* ● *Hardware independence* ● *Variable costs* ● *Time to market* ● *Distribution over the Internet*	
● Scalability	Lesson 2, Topic B
● Types of Scalability	Lesson 2, Topic B
● Scalability with Different Types of Cloud	Lesson 2, Topic B
● Security	Lesson 2, Topic C
● Security Concerns	Lesson 2, Topic C
● Security Features in Cloud	Lesson 2, Topic C
● Customizing Security in the Cloud	Lesson 2, Topic C
● Variable Costs	Lesson 2, Topic D
● Time to Market	Lesson 2, Topic D
● Distribution over the Internet	Lesson 2, Topic D

Exam Objective	Cloud Essentials Certification Lesson and Topic Reference
2.3 Demonstrate how the characteristics of cloud computing enhance business value.	
● Level of Value Provided by Cloud	Lesson 2, Topic D
● Utility Level - Basic Level	Lesson 2, Topic D
● Process Transformation Level - Intermediate Level	Lesson 2, Topic D

Exam Objective	Cloud Essentials Certification Lesson and Topic Reference
2.3 Demonstrate how the characteristics of cloud computing enhance business value.	
● Business Model Innovation - Advanced Level	Lesson 2, Topic D
● Business Drivers for Migrating to Cloud	Lesson 2, Topic A
● SME Business and Cloud Computing	Lesson 2, Topic A
● Large Business and Cloud Computing	Lesson 2, Topic A
● Start-up Business and Cloud Computing	Lesson 2, Topic A

Exam Objective	Cloud Essentials Certification Lesson and Topic Reference
Domain 3.0 Technical Perspectives/Cloud Types	
3.1 Understand the difference between private and public types of clouds from a technical perspective and provide examples.	
Understand the difference between private and public types of clouds from a technical perspective and provide examples.	Lesson 3, Topic A

Exam Objective	Cloud Essentials Certification Lesson and Topic Reference
3.2 Understand at a high level the following important techniques and methods for cloud computing deployment:	
● Networking	Lesson 3, Topic B
● Automation and Self-Service	Lesson 3, Topic C
● Federation	Lesson 3, Topic D
● The role of standardization	Lesson 3, Topic E

Exam Objective	Cloud Essentials Certification Lesson and Topic Reference
3.3 Explain technical challenges and risks for cloud computing and methods to mitigate them for:	
● Cloud storage	Lesson 4, Topic A
● Application performance	Lesson 4, Topic B
● Data integration	Lesson 4, Topic C
● Security	Lesson 4, Topic D

Exam Objective	Cloud Essentials Certification Lesson and Topic Reference
3.4 Describe the impact of cloud computing on application architecture and the application-development process.	
Describe the impact of cloud computing on application architecture and the application-development process.	Lesson 4, Topic E

Exam Objective	Cloud Essentials Certification Lesson and Topic Reference
Domain 4.0 Steps to Successful Adoption of Cloud	
4.1 Explain typical steps that lead to a successful adoption of cloud computing services:	
• Understand selection criteria for a pilot	Lesson 5, Topic
• Relate SaaS, PaaS, IaaS deployment to organizational goals	Lesson 5, Topic

Exam Objective	Cloud Essentials Certification Lesson and Topic Reference
4.2 Understand the roles and capabilities of cloud computing vendors and dependencies on the vendors.	
Understand the roles and capabilities of cloud computing vendors and dependencies on the vendors.	Lesson 5, Topic C

Exam Objective	Cloud Essentials Certification Lesson and Topic Reference
4.3 Understand the following organizational capabilities that are relevant for realizing cloud benefits:	
• Skills that are required in an organization adopting cloud computing • Critical success factors	Lesson 5, Topic

Exam Objective	Cloud Essentials Certification Lesson and Topic Reference
4.4 Describe multiple approaches for migrating applications.	
Describe multiple approaches for migrating applications.	Lesson 5, Topic D

Exam Objective	Cloud Essentials Certification Lesson and Topic Reference
Domain 5.0 Impact and Changes of Cloud Computing on IT Service Management	
5.1 Understand the impact and changes cloud computing on IT service management in a typical organization: ● **Service Strategy** ● **Service Design** ● **Service Operation** ● **Service Transition**	
● Service Management	Lesson 6, Topic A
● ITSM	Lesson 6, Topic A
■ ITIL	Lesson 6, Topic A
● The Service Lifecycle	Lesson 6, Topic A
■ Service Strategy	Lesson 6, Topic A Lesson 6, Topic B
● Service Design	Lesson 6, Topic A Lesson 6, Topic C
■ Service Transition	Lesson 6, Topic A Lesson 6, Topic D
■ Service Operation	Lesson 6, Topic A Lesson 6, Topic E
■ Continual Service Improvement	Lesson 6, Topic A Lesson 6, Topic F

Exam Objective	Cloud Essentials Certification Lesson and Topic Reference
5.2 Use a structured approach based on ITIL to explore the potential impact of cloud computing in your organization.	
● Portfolio Management	Lesson 6, Topic B
■ Demand Management	Lesson 6, Topic B
■ Financial Management	Lesson 6, Topic B
■ How to Adopt Service Strategy for Cloud Services	Lesson 6, Topic B
● Service Catalog	Lesson 6, Topic C
■ Service Catalog Management	Lesson 6, Topic C
■ Service Level Management	Lesson 6, Topic C
■ Availability Management	Lesson 6, Topic C

Exam Objective	Cloud Essentials Certification Lesson and Topic Reference
5.2 Use a structured approach based on ITIL to explore the potential impact of cloud computing in your organization.	
■ Capacity Management	Lesson 6, Topic C
■ IT Service Continuity Management	Lesson 6, Topic C
■ Information Security Management	Lesson 6, Topic C
■ The IT Security Framework	Lesson 6, Topic C
■ Supplier Management	Lesson 6, Topic C
■ Impact of Poor Cloud Service Design	Lesson 6, Topic C
● Service Design Considerations	Lesson 6, Topic C
■ Change Management	Lesson 6, Topic D
■ Service Asset and Configuration Management	Lesson 6, Topic D
■ Release and Deployment Management	Lesson 6, Topic D
■ Service Validation and Testing	Lesson 6, Topic D
● Service Evaluation	Lesson 6, Topic D
● Knowledge Management	Lesson 6, Topic D
● How To Transition to Cloud	Lesson 6, Topic D
■ Service Desk	Lesson 6, Topic E
■ Incident	Lesson 6, Topic E
■ Incident Lifecycle	Lesson 6, Topic E
■ Incident Management	Lesson 6, Topic E
■ Problem	Lesson 6, Topic E
■ Problem Management	Lesson 6, Topic E
● Request Fulfilment	Lesson 6, Topic E
■ Access Management	Lesson 6, Topic E
■ Event Management	Lesson 6, Topic E
● Technical Management	Lesson 6, Topic E
● IT Operations Management	Lesson 6, Topic E
● Application Management	Lesson 6, Topic E
● How to Mitigate Risks involved in Operating Cloud Services	Lesson 6, Topic E
■ Service Reporting	Lesson 6, Topic F
■ Service Measurement	Lesson 6, Topic F
● The CSI Model	Lesson 6, Topic F
● Seven Steps of the CSI Process	Lesson 6, Topic F

Exam Objective	Cloud Essentials Certification Lesson and Topic Reference
Domain 6.0 Risks and Consequences of Cloud Computing	
6.1 Explain and identify the issues associated with integrating cloud computing into an organization's existing compliance risk and regulatory framework:	
● Risk Analysis	Lesson 7, Topic A
● Risk Management	Lesson 7, Topic A
● Organizational Risks	Lesson 7, Topic A
● Vendor Lock-In	Lesson 7, Topic A
● Loss of Management Control	Lesson 7, Topic A
● Compliance with Regulations	Lesson 7, Topic A
● Lack of Resources	Lesson 7, Topic A
● Failure of Cloud Services	Lesson 7, Topic A
● Failure of the Supply Chain	Lesson 7, Topic A
● Incorrect or Incompatible Service Level Agreements	Lesson 7, Topic A
● Security Legal	Lesson 7, Topic B
● Compliance	Lesson 7, Topic C

Exam Objective	Cloud Essentials Certification Lesson and Topic Reference
6.2 Explain the implications for direct costs and cost allocations.	
● Direct Cost vs. Indirect Cost	Lesson 7, Topic D
■ Total Cost of Ownership	Lesson 7, Topic D
■ Impact of Indirect Costs on TCO	Lesson 7, Topic D
● TCO for SaaS, PaaS and IaaS	Lesson 7, Topic D
● Return on Investment (ROI)	Lesson 7, Topic D

Exam Objective	Cloud Essentials Certification Lesson and Topic Reference
6.3 Understand how to maintain strategic flexibility.	
Understand how to maintain strategic flexibility.	Lesson 7, Topic E

B | CompTIA® Cloud Essentials™ (Exam CLO-001) Acronyms

The following is a list of acronyms that appear in the CompTIA® Cloud Essentials™ (Exam CLO-001) course. Candidates are encouraged to review the complete list and attain a working knowledge of all listed acronyms as a part of a comprehensive exam preparation program.

Acronym	Associated Term
ALM	Application Lifecycle Management
APM	Application Performance Management
API	Application Programming Interface
AWS	Amazon Web Services
BCM	Business Continuity Management
BSM	Business Service Management
CAPEX	Capital Expenditure
CAPTCHA	Completely Automated Public Turing test to tell Computers and Humans Apart
CAB	Change Advisory Board
CCIF	Cloud Computing Interoperability Forum
CCTA	Central Computer and Telecommunications Agency
CDN	Content Delivery Network
CMDB	Configuration Management Database
CSI	Continual Service Improvement
CSA	Cloud Security Alliance
CWE	Common Weaknesses Enumeration
OPEX	Operational Expenditure
DBMS	Database Management System
DBaaS	Database as a Service
DDoS	Distributed Denial of Service
DFS	Distributed File System
3 DES	3-Data Encryption Standards

Acronym	Associated Term
EDoS	Economic Denial of Sustainability
HVAC	Heat, Ventilation, and Air Condition
HIPAA	Health Insurance Portability and Accountability Act
IaaS	Infrastructure as a Service
ID-FF	Identity Federation Framework
ISMS	Information Security Management System
ITSM	IT Service Management
IT	Information Technology
ITIL	IT Infrastructure Library
KPI	Key Performance Indicators
MitM	Man-in-the-Middle
NVD	National Vulnerability Database
NIST	National Institute of Standards and Technology
OLA	Operational Level Agreement
OSA	Open Security Architecture
OSI	Open Systems Interconnection
PaaS	Platform as a Service
PCI	Payment Card Industry
PDCA	Plan-Do-Check-Act
RFC	Request for Change
ROI	Return on Investment
RDS	Relational Database Service
ROA	Return On Assets
SaaS	Software as a Service
SAS	Statement on Auditing Standards
SACM	Service Asset and Configuration Management
SCM	Service Catalog Management
SCD	Supplier and Contract Database
SLA	Service Level Agreement
SLR	Service Level Requirement
SME	Small to Medium Enterprise
SOA	Service-Oriented Architecture
SSL	Secure Sockets Layer
UC	Underpinning Contract
VF	Virtual Firewall
VPN	Virtual Private Network
VXLAN	Virtual eXtensible Local Area Network
VPC	Virtual Private Cloud
TCP	Transmission Control Protocol
TCO	Total Cost of Ownership

Lesson Labs

Lesson labs are provided as an additional learning resource for this course. The labs may or may not be performed as part of the classroom activities. Your instructor will consider setup issues, classroom timing issues, and instructional needs to determine which labs are appropriate for you to perform, and at what point during the class. If you do not perform the labs in class, your instructor can tell you if you can perform them independently as self-study, and if there are any special setup requirements.

Lesson 1 Lab 1

Introduction to Cloud Computing

Data Files:

Crossword_L1_Starter.png, Crossword_Starter.htm

Scenario:

In this activity, you will identify the fundamentals of cloud services. It is essential that you complete the lesson to successfully perform the crossword.

1. Navigate to the C:\085195Data\Introduction to Cloud Computing folder to open the Crossword_Starter.htm file.

2. Print the Crossword_Starter.htm and the Crossword_L1_Starter.png files.

3. Read the descriptions in the **Across** and **Down** sections and fill the answers in the grid of the Crossword_L1_Starter.png file.

4. Open the Crossword_Solution.htm file and compare it to your answers.

Lesson 2 Lab 1

Business Value of Cloud Computing

Data Files:

Crossword_L2_Starter.png, Crossword_Starter.htm

Scenario:

In this activity, you will identify the business value of cloud services. It is essential that you complete the lesson to successfully perform the crossword.

1. Navigate to the C:\085195Data\Business Value of Cloud folder to open the Crossword_ Starter.htm file.

2. Print the Crossword_Starter.htm and the Crossword_L2_Starter.png files.

3. Read the descriptions in the **Across** and **Down** sections and fill the answers in the grid of the Crossword_L2_Starter.png file.

4. Open the Crossword_Solution.htm file and compare it to your answers.

Lesson 3 Lab 1
Technical Perspectives of Cloud Computing

Data Files:

Crossword_L3_Starter.png, Crossword_Starter.htm

Scenario:

In this activity, you will identify the various cloud types, and the means to deploy the cloud services. It is essential that you complete the lesson to successfully perform the crossword.

1. Navigate to the C:\085195Data\Technical Perspectives of Cloud folder to open the Crossword_Starter.htm file.

2. Print the Crossword_Starter.htm file.

3. Read the descriptions in the **Across** and **Down** sections and fill the answers in the grid.

4. Open the Crossword_Solution.htm file and compare it to your answers.

Lesson 4 Lab 1

Technical Challenges of Cloud Computing

Data Files:

Crossword_Starter.htm, Crossword_L4_Starter.png

Scenario:

In this activity, you will examine the technical challenges of adopting cloud services and the mitigation measures to follow. It is essential that you complete the lesson to successfully perform the crossword.

---

1. Navigate to the C:\085195Data\Technical Challenges of Cloud Computing folder to open the Crossword_Starter.htm file.

---

2. Print the Crossword_Starter.htm file.

---

3. Read the descriptions in the **Across** and **Down** sections and fill the answers in the grid of the Crossword_L4_Starter.png file.

---

4. Open the Crossword_Solution.htm file and compare it to your answers.

Lesson 5 Lab 1

Steps to Successful Adoption of Cloud Services

Data Files:

Crossword_L5_Starter.png, Crossword_Starter.htm

Scenario:

In this activity, you will identify the steps to successfully adopt cloud services. It is essential that you complete the lesson to successfully perform the crossword.

---

1. Navigate to the C:\085195Data\Steps to Successful Adoption of Cloud Services folder to open the Crossword_Starter.htm file.

---

2. Print the Crossword_Starter.htm and the Crossword_L5_Starter.png files.

3. Read the descriptions in the **Across** and **Down** sections and fill the answers in the grid of the Crossword_L5_Starter.png file.

4. Open the Crossword_Solution.htm and compare it to your answers.

Lesson 6 Lab 1
Examining the Fundamentals of ITIL and Cloud Computing

Data Files:

Crossword_L6_01_Starter.png, Crossword_Starter_01.htm

Scenario:

In this activity, you will examine the fundamentals of ITIL and cloud computing. It is essential that you complete this course to successfully perform the crossword.

1. Navigate to the C:\085195Data\ITIL and Cloud Computing folder to open the Crossword_Starter_01.htm file.

2. Print the Crossword_Starter_01.htm and the Crossword_L6_01_Starter.png files.

3. Read the descriptions in the **Across** and **Down** sections and fill the answers in the grid of the Crossword_L6_01_Starter.png file.

4. Open the Crossword_Solution_01.htm file and compare it to your answers.

Lesson 6 Lab 2

Examining the Fundamentals of ITIL and Cloud Computing

Data Files:

Crossword_L6_02_Starter.png, Crossword_Starter_02.htm

Scenario:

In this activity, you will examine the fundamentals of ITIL and cloud computing. It is essential that you complete the lesson to successfully perform the crossword.

1. Navigate to the C:\085195Data\ITIL and Cloud Computing folder to open the Crossword_ Starter_02.htm file.

2. Print the Crossword_Starter_01.htm and the Crossword_L6_02_Starter.png files.

3. Read the descriptions in the **Across** and **Down** sections and fill the answers in the grid of the Crossword_L6_02_Starter.png file.

4. Open the Crossword_Solution_02.htm file and compare it to your answers.

Lesson 7 Lab 1

Identifying Risks and Risk Mitigation Measures

Scenario:

You have identified ITIL standards that can be implemented when employing cloud services in your organization. You need to be proactive and take every step possible to deploy cloud services successfully.

1. **What is the objective of Risk Management?**

   a) Support transfer of data and application to another vendor.

   b) Prevent access by unauthorized users by effective and easy personal identity management.

   c) Involves the identification, selection, and adoption of countermeasures in a way that is most appropriate to the identified risks.

   d) Evaluate all the aspects of data portability before migration to cloud.

2. **What are the security risk factors for Vendor Lock-in? Choose all that apply.**

   a) No assurance for the data, application, and service portability in a cloud.

   b) Consumer is dependent on the cloud provider and may face challenges if the cloud provider is out of business.

   c) Data and application migration to another provider proves too costly and time consuming.

   d) Illegal data access by co-tenants and poor quality of service.

3. **What is a Virtual Machine?**

   a) An interface that describes the syntax of the operations supported by the system.

   b) A file (typically called an image) which, when executed, appears like an actual machine to the user.

   c) It is an open standard for authentication that allows users to share private resources such as photos, videos or contact lists without sharing user credentials.

   d) A virtualizer which maps physical resources to virtualized resources.

Lesson 7 Lab 2
Identifying Risks Factors and Mitigation Measures

Data Files:

Crossword_L7_Starter.png, Crossword_Starter.htm

Scenario:

In this activity, you will examine various risk factors associated with adapting to cloud services, and the measures to mitigate them. It is essential that you complete the lesson to successfully perform the crossword.

1. Navigate to the C:\085195Data\Identifying Risks and Consequences folder to open the Crossword_Starter.htm file.

2. Print the Crossword_Starter.htm and the Crossword_L7_Starter.png files.

3. Read the descriptions in the **Across** and **Down** sections and fill the answers in the grid of the Crossword_L7_Starter.png file.

4. Open the Crossword_Solution.htm file and compare it to your answers.

Solutions

Lesson 1

Activity 1-1

1. **Which component is a set of programming instructions and standards for accessing a web-based program?**

   a) Platform

   ✓ b) Web API

   c) Web Browser

   d) Web Application

2. **Identify the client that uses a web browser as an interface to connect to the cloud.**

   ✓ a) Thick

   b) Thin

   c) Mobile

   d) Web API

Activity 1-2

1. **Which model facilitates sharing of a complex computational task across multiple computers?**

   a) Client-Server

   b) Peer-to-Peer

   ✓ c) Grid Computing

   d) Virtualization

2. **True or False? All applications accessed through the Internet are cloud applications.**

   ___ True

   ✓ False

Activity 1-3

1. **What are the benefits of DBaaS? (Choose all that apply.)**

   ✓ a) Higher availability of resources

   ✓ b) Better service

   ✓ c) Reduced risks

      d) High costs

2. **True or False? Distributed computing helps to perform data-intensive tasks for applications.**

   ✓ True

   __ False

Lesson 2

Activity 2-1

1. **What are the business drivers of cloud computing? (Choose all that apply.)**

      a) Increased time to market

   ✓ b) Cost efficiencies maximization

   ✓ c) Strategic planning

   ✓ d) Accommodation of unpredictable demand

2. **True or False? SaaS provides services to an organization that requires the standard business process infrastructure such as CRM.**

   ✓ True

   __ False

Activity 2-2

1. **Which type of scaling involves the addition of additional processors, RAM, or disk space to a server?**

      a) Load Balancing

   ✓ b) Vertical Scaling

      c) Horizontal Scaling

      d) Diagonal Scaling

2. **True or False? Scalability provides a flexible infrastructure architecture to software organizations.**

   ✓ True

   __ False

Activity 2-3

1. **What are the major security concerns with regard to cloud computing? (Choose all that apply.)**

    a) Data integration

    ✓ b) Data location

    ✓ c) Recovery

    ✓ d) Long-term viability

2. **True or False? Cloud security is deployed to protect data, applications, and the infrastructure of cloud computing.**

    ✓ True

    ___ False

Activity 2-4

1. **At which level does an organization benefit through the availability of elastic computing resources and pay-per-use models of cloud computing?**

    ✓ a) Utility

    b) Process Transformation

    c) Business Model Innovation

    d) Smart Metering

2. **What are the elements of an organization that are deployed at the Utility level? (Choose all that apply.)**

    ✓ a) Labor

    ✓ b) Software

    ✓ c) Hardware

    d) Business Model

Lesson 3

Activity 3-1

1. **Which deployment model provides cloud services to a limited number of people within an organization?**

    a) Public cloud service

    ✓ b) Private cloud service

    c) Community cloud service

    d) Hybrid cloud service

2. **True or False? When costs are being shared among fewer users, public cloud computing is a more expensive venture.**

___ True

✓ False

Activity 3-2

1. **What are the essential components of a cloud network? (Choose all that apply.)**

   a) Scalability

   ✓ b) Hypervisor

   c) Latency

   ✓ d) Storage

   ✓ e) Operating System

2. **True or False? Network node latency can be reduced by using optimized fabric.**

   ✓ True

   ___ False

Activity 3-3

1. **What are the key benefits of cloud automation? (Choose all that apply.)**

   ✓ a) Optimal utilization of the cloud resources

   ✓ b) Minimal cost incurred for maintenance (power consumption)

   c) High operating costs

   ✓ d) Adherence to compliance standards for data security

2. **True or False? User authentication is the basic attribute of self-service.**

   ✓ True

   ___ False

Activity 3-4

1. **True or False? The use of pseudonyms is not encouraged in user identity management systems of a federated cloud environment because it is a breach of trust.**

   ___ True

   ✓ False

2. **What are the chief characteristics of the Cloud Gateway? (Choose all that apply.)**

   a) Data resiliency

   ✓ b) Data backup

   ✓ c) Cloud cache

   ✓ d) Provisioning of network resources

Activity 3-5

1. **True or False? Interoperability in federated cloud reduces the need for vendor lock-in.**

    _✓_ True

    ___ False

2. **What are the various standards adopted by the service providers to ensure the security of data in a federated cloud environment? (Choose all that apply.)**

    ✓ a) Cloud Security Alliance

    ✓ b) The Green Grid

    ✓ c) SAS 70

        d) Cloud Computing interoperability forum

Lesson 4

Activity 4-1

1. **Identify the challenges involved in cloud service backup. (Choose all that apply.)**

    ✓ a) Bandwidth

    ✓ b) Security

        c) Reliability

    ✓ d) Recovery

2. **True or False? In cloud computing, there is a trade-off between reliability and the speed of deployment.**

    _✓_ True

    ___ False

Activity 4-2

1. **Identify the challenges involved in performance management of cloud applications. (Choose all that apply.)**

    ✓ a) Monitoring operating systems

    ✓ b) Monitoring databases

    ✓ c) Monitoring servers

        d) Monitoring usage

2. **Identify the benefits of cloud databases. (Choose Three)**

   a) Improved security

   ✓ b) Increased accessibility

   ✓ c) Automated scalability

   ✓ d) Minimal investment

Activity 4-3

1. **Identify the challenges involved in data integration. (Choose all that apply.)**

   ✓ a) Speed of change

   ✓ b) Data distribution

   ✓ c) Data volumes

   d) Data privacy

2. **Identify the challenges involved in migrating data to the cloud.**

   ✓ a) Liability

   ✓ b) Data protection

   c) Data distribution

   ✓ d) Data interruption

Activity 4-4

1. **Identify the challenges involved in implementing cloud security. (Choose all that apply.)**

   a) Scalability

   ✓ b) Security controls

   ✓ c) Sharing of resources

   ✓ d) Loss of control

2. **True or False? PCI is not a specific set of auditing standards; instead, cloud providers are responsible for choosing their own controls and the goals those controls intend to achieve.**

   ___ True

   ✓ False

Activity 4-5

1. **True or False? The traditional architecture is designed to balance heavy work load in the cloud.**

   ___ True

   ✓ False

2. **Identify the architecture that splits the workload over multiple servers to improve processing power.**

    a) Traditional application

    b) Scale-up

✓ c) Scale-out

    d) Multi-tier application

Lesson 5

Activity 5-1

1. **Identify the feature that helps you determine the level of service provided by the cloud vendor.**

    a) Historical performance

✓ b) Redundancy

    c) Monitoring

    d) SLA

2. **What is the first step involved in the vendor selection process?**

    a) Drawing an outline with the critical criteria that determines the desired cloud vendor.

✓ b) Analyzing the organization.

    c) Comparing cloud vendors based on the selected criteria.

    d) Finalizing the cloud vendor.

Activity 5-2

1. **Identify the activities that help you determine cloud readiness. (Choose all that apply.)**

✓ a) Optimize the current environment by providing an internal set of cloud services and enabling the incorporation of external services.

    b) Draft the Service Level Agreement (SLA).

✓ c) Designate a cross-functional team to monitor cloud services.

✓ d) Undertake pilot projects with various services.

2. **What are the tasks involved in drafting a plan for cloud migration? (Choose all that apply.)**

✓ a) Run "what-if" analysis to make build vs. buy cloud computing decisions such as on-premise private cloud, hosted private cloud, and public cloud.

✓ b) Determine cost and value trade-offs of your cloud computing architectures.

✓ c) Design and manage cloud performance KPIs such as unit rate reduction goals and return on assets (ROA).

    d) Analyze the organization.

Activity 5-3

1. **Identify ways to minimize threats to data integrity. (Choose all that apply.)**

   a) Determine how well the vendor meets your detailed requirements.

   ✓ b) Back up data regularly.

   ✓ c) Control access to data using security mechanisms.

   ✓ d) Design user interfaces that prevent the input of invalid data.

2. **True or False? The externalized aspect of outsourcing makes it harder to maintain data integrity and privacy.**

   ✓ True

   ___ False

Activity 5-4

1. **Identify the cloud migration pattern that is most appropriate for the separation of application logic and database components in the current application.**

   a) Service facade pattern

   b) Re-host and optimize

   ✓ c) Application re-hosting

   d) Re-architect

2. **Identify the degree of multi-tenancy that allows the database schema to be shared and supports customization of the business logic and user-interface layers.**

   a) Lowest

   b) Middle

   ✓ c) Highest

Lesson 6

Activity 6-1

1. **Which Lifecycle phase is concerned with building and testing a service before it is delivered to the customers?**

   a) Service Design

   b) Service Operation

   ✓ c) Service Transition

   d) Continual Service Improvement

2. **Which Lifecycle phase is concerned with financial planning?**

   a) Service Design

   ✓ b) Service Strategy

   c) Service Operation

   d) Service Planning

3. **Which phase is a larger, all-encompassing phase in the IT Service Lifecycle that can be applied at any point in the Lifecycle?**

   a) Service Transition

   b) Service Measurement

   c) Service Design

   ✓ d) Continual Service Improvement

4. **Which Lifecycle phase consists of processes and functions that are required for the service to be provided at the agreed-upon service level?**

   a) Service Design

   ✓ b) Service Operation

   c) Service Transition

   d) Service Strategy

Activity 6-2

1. **Identify the three different phases of Service Strategy.**

   ✓ a) Portfolio Management

   ✓ b) Demand Management

   c) Change Management

   ✓ d) Financial Management

2. **What is the overall goal of demand management?**

   a) To determine the best possible use of its monetary resources to provide services.

   ✓ b) To determine a balance between the offering of a service and the demand for that service.

   c) To deliver and support operational IT services to achieve business and deliver forecasted business benefits.

   d) To deliver service value by facilitating the desired outcome that customers want to achieve.

3. **Who also should be included in making service strategy decisions along with the cloud providers?**

   a) Capacity Manager

   b) IT Staff

   ✓ c) Consumer Business Managers

   d) Security Manager

4. **Identify the risks that are involved in the three stages of Service Strategy.**

 ✓ a) Failure to identify the specific delivery model of cloud will result in service delays when fixing incidents and problems.

 b) Failure to provide services and meet demands ahead of time.

 ✓ c) Failure to measure the demand exactly could result in agreed demand levels going beyond and penalties being imposed by the cloud suppliers.

 ✓ d) Failure to specify and measure performance requirements during peak periods could result in unwarranted delays for users of cloud-based services.

Activity 6-3

1. **Match each management process with its corresponding example.**

_b_	Information Security Management	a.	Single points of failure are removed from the infrastructure in order to add resiliency.
_d_	Capacity Management	b.	Databases containing financial data are available to employees within the finance department only.
_e_	Supplier Management	c.	The IT department audits its service to ensure that all documented service hours, contact numbers, and Service Level Agreements (SLAs) are correct.
_a_	Availability Management	d.	The number of users for this service is expected to double over the next two years.
_c_	Service Catalog Management	e.	A plan is put into place for an Internet service provider (ISP) whose performance was below expectations last quarter.

2. **Which of the following is an internal agreement between the support teams of an IT service provider?**

 a) Department Support Agreement

 b) Service Level Agreement

 c) IT Support Agreement

 ✓ d) Operational Level Agreement

3. **True or False? The ability of an organization to restore Service Operations after a catastrophic failure is the goal of availability management.**

 ___ True

 ✓ False

4. **Samuel establishes a formal agreement with a client to set up the service hours of operation, transaction response times, and throughput expectations. This activity is part of which process of the Service Design Phase?**

 a) Availability Management

 b) Capacity Management

 ✓ c) Service Level Management

 d) Supplier Management

Activity 6-4

1. **Which of the following is an objective of the Service Transition phase?**

   a) To develop strategies on what the business needs, and what it does not.

   b) To develop a strategy for restoring normal service operation as quickly as possible following a disruption.

   c) To continually realign IT services to changing business needs.

   ✓ d) To plan and manage the resources to establish a new or changed service into production within constraints.

2. **Which of the following processes of the Service Transition phase manages the building, testing, and delivering of new or changed service components?**

   a) Change management

   b) SACM

   ✓ c) Release and deployment management

   d) Knowledge management

Activity 6-5

1. **Which of the following is the best example of an incident?**

   a) A DNS Server has had its IP address changed.

   b) A user logs on to her workstation.

   ✓ c) A customer attempts to place an order through your company website, and the transaction gets caught in a loop and never completes.

   d) A network drive has reached 65% capacity, which is within the boundaries of the SLA.

2. **Which of the following is the best example of a problem?**

   a) A customer is unable to log on to her account, even after entering her user name and password correctly.

   b) An unauthorized attempt to access the wireless network was blocked.

   ✓ c) No one can access a database, and it's discovered that the password database is offline, but the reason for the database to go offline is unknown.

3. **Which of the following occurs in the financial authorization activity of the Request Fulfilment process? Choose all that apply.**

   ✓ a) Determining a cost prior to handling the request.

   b) Verifying that the user's budget allows for the request to be made.

   ✓ c) Determining the cost after a user makes a request.

   d) Determining that the request falls within your fulfilment budget.

Activity 6-6

1. **Match the step in the CSI Model with its definition.**

_b_	What is the vision?	a.	Choose measurable, achievable targets. How do you want to measure your target level of improvement?
_d_	Where are we now?	b.	Formulate a vision, define the mission, create goals, and make objectives that work together with the business.
_a_	Where do we want to be?	c.	Create a detailed SIP, an outline of specific steps to be taken to improve the service.
_c_	How do we get there?	d.	Record a baseline. What is the current level of performance?
_f_	Did we get there?	e.	Any change worth keeping is absorbed to be maintained.
_e_	How do we keep the momentum going?	f.	See if the objectives have been met, and whether the processes have been complied. This step is measurable and objective.

2. **During which step of the CSI Process Model are stakeholders informed about whether or not goals have been achieved?**

   a) Process data

   ✓ b) Present and use information

   c) Implement corrective action

   d) Analyze data

Lesson 7

Activity 7-1

1. **What happens to cloud providers when they face a new market technology, competitive pressure, an inadequate business strategy, or lack of financial support?**

   ✓ a) They run out of business, lose their services or restructure their business services.

   b) They look for more financial support.

   c) They allocate new resources.

   d) They cancel the SLAs.

2. **Name the security risk factors associated with the delivery model of cloud services. (Choose Three.)**

   a) Scalability

   ✓ b) Loss of management control

   ✓ c) Lock-in

   ✓ d) Compliance regulations

Activity 7-2

1. **True or False? In a public cloud, service providers give complete assurance for data security.**

   ___ True

   ✓ False

2. **When does an organization become prone to a man-in-the-middle attack?**

   a) When there is a denial of service.

   b) When there is a loss of encryption keys.

   ✓ c) When there is interception of data in transit.

Activity 7-3

1. **What are the legislation risks involved while adopting cloud services? (Choose all that apply.)**

   ✓ a) Data permanence

   ✓ b) Jurisdiction issues

   c) High cost and latency

   ✓ d) Lawful access

2. **True or False? Online licensing checks help ensure the availability of software licenses when adopting cloud services.**

   ___ True

   ✓ False

Activity 7-4

1. **Identify the indirect costs that affect TCO in an organization.**

   ✓ a) Security.

   b) Value-added services.

   ✓ c) Scalability.

   ✓ d) Interoperability.

2. **What is the correct definition of TCO?**

   a) TCO provides value added services to a customer.

   b) TCO identifies only the intangible costs associated with a product or system.

   ✓ c) TCO is a cost calculation designed to evaluate direct and indirect costs of a product or system.

   d) TCO is a performance metric used to measure the efficiency of an investment.

3. **Identify the various cost factors for an IaaS cloud provider. (Choose all that apply.)**

   ✓ a) No server maintenance costs.

   ✓ b) No ongoing IT support costs or operation costs involved.

   c) No outsourcing of IT infrastructure.

   ✓ d) Low subscription fees for the IT help desk.

Activity 7-5

1. **True or False? Organizations with defined demand levels can adopt public cloud services as their demand for resources is always constant.**

   __ True

   ✓ False

2. **What compliance and governance requirements should be ascertained by organizations before opting for cloud services? (Choose all that apply.)**

   ✓ a) Audit

   b) Monitoring the cloud model

   ✓ c) Detection and Forensics

   ✓ d) Encryption Standards

Lesson 7 Follow-up

Lesson 7 Lab 1

1. **What is the objective of Risk Management?**

   a) Support transfer of data and application to another vendor.

   b) Prevent access by unauthorized users by effective and easy personal identity management.

   ✓ c) Involves the identification, selection, and adoption of countermeasures in a way that is most appropriate to the identified risks.

   d) Evaluate all the aspects of data portability before migration to cloud.

2. **What are the security risk factors for Vendor Lock-in? Choose all that apply.**

   ✓ a) No assurance for the data, application, and service portability in a cloud.

   ✓ b) Consumer is dependent on the cloud provider and may face challenges if the cloud provider is out of business.

   ✓ c) Data and application migration to another provider proves too costly and time consuming.

   d) Illegal data access by co-tenants and poor quality of service.

3. What is a Virtual Machine?

    a) An interface that describes the syntax of the operations supported by the system.

✓ b) A file (typically called an image) which, when executed, appears like an actual machine to the user.

    c) It is an open standard for authentication that allows users to share private resources such as photos, videos or contact lists without sharing user credentials.

    d) A virtualizer which maps physical resources to virtualized resources.

Glossary

Access Management
The process that grants authorized users access to the use of an IT service along with the rights to which functions of a service they can utilize. It includes verification of identity and entitlement, grant of access to services, log and track access, and remove or modify rights when status or roles change.

Application Management
A management process that includes the management of software applications by the lines of business that each team supports.

ARIMA
(Auto-Regressive Integrated Moving Average) A model that helps in forecasting a time series by transformations such as differencing and logging.

asset management
The process responsible for tracking and reporting the value and ownership of financial assets throughout their lifecycle. Asset management is part of the overall SACM process.

authentication issues
A process where a user is identified and provided authentication to log on to the system.

Automation
is a system followed by the service providers to offer, deliver, manage, and bill for the rendered services.

Availability Management
A process that outlines the measures you can take to ensure that the customers have steady access to the services they require.

BSM
(Business Service Management) An approach to the management of IT services that considers the supported business processes and the provided business value. This term also means the management of business services delivered to business customers.

Business Capacity Management
In the context of ITSM, Business Capacity Management is the activity responsible for understanding future business requirements for use in the capacity plan.

Business Model Innovation level
The advanced level at which an organization creates new business models by linking, sharing, and combining resources using cloud computing in an entire business ecosystem.

CAB
(Change Advisory Board) A panel of personnel who convene on a regular basis to help the Change Manager assess, prioritize, and schedule any necessary changes to one or more IT services.

Cache as a Service
A type of cloud service that speeds up dynamic web applications by alleviating the database load.

Caching
A process of buffering the frequently accessed data in order to speed up the process of information retrieval.

Capacity Management
The process of delivering quality IT services for agreed upon service level targets at an optimum cost.

change management
The process responsible for controlling the lifecycle of all changes. The primary objective of change management is to enable beneficial changes to be made, with minimal disruption to IT services.

client-server model
A network in which some nodes act as servers to provide special services on behalf of other client nodes.

client
An interface with which a user or another application accesses cloud services.

Cloud computing
Cloud computing is a business model that delivers software, infrastructure, and hardware facilities over the network based on user demand. This is a pay-per-use model that helps an organization to use the resources as and when needed and pay only for the facilities used.

Cluster
A cluster is a group of systems that are coupled together, generally via a fast network, so they are aware of each other.

CMDB
(configuration management database) A database that is used to store the configuration records and attributes of a CI. Typically, the Configuration Management System is built from one or more CMDBs.

Community cloud
A cloud solution that enables sharing of resources within organizations having similar requirements.

Component Capacity Management
The process responsible for understanding the capacity, utilization, and performance of configuration items. Data is collected, recorded, and analyzed for use in the capacity plan.

Configuration Management System (CMS)
A set of tools and databases that are used to manage an IT service provider's configuration data. The CMS is maintained by configuration management and is used by all IT service management processes.

configuration management
The process responsible for maintaining information about the CIs required to deliver an IT service, including their relationships. Configuration management is part of the overall SACM process.

continual service improvement
A phase in the IT Service Lifecycle that is responsible for managing improvements to IT service management processes and IT services to increase efficiency, effectiveness, and cost effectiveness.

cross-site scripting (XSS)
A process where a site validates, filters, or encodes user input before returning it to another user's web client.

CSFs
(critical success factor) An element that is essential for achieving the business mission of a service. CSFs can either be qualitative or quantitative. KPIs are used to measure each CSF.

database profiler
A process of collecting statistics and information about data available in a data source.

Database-as-a-Service
See DBaaS.

DBaaS
(Database-as-a-Service) A type of cloud service that allows organizations to leverage hardware and software solutions that involve databases.

DDoS attack

(Distributed Denial of Service attack) An attempt by which a person prevents the intended users from utilizing a service hosted on a site.

demand management

A process of the Service Strategy phase that balances the supply of a service to the demand for the service.

deployment

The activity responsible for the movement of new or changed hardware, software, documentation, processes, etc. to the live environment.

DFS

(Distributed file system) A file system that allows access to files from multiple computers that are shared via network.

direct cost

A cost for an activity or service than can be charged to a specific project or customer.

Distributed computing

A web service that performs a consolidated function by involving number of computers that are remotely placed, and connected in a network.

Distributed database

A database in which storage devices are stored in multiple computers located in the same physical location, or may be dispersed over a network.

Distributed file system

See DFS.

EDoS attack

(Economic Denial of Sustainability attack). An attempt by the cloud service providers disallows an organization to utilize the hardware resources of the cloud.

emulator

Hardware or software or both that duplicates the functions of one computer system in another computer system, so that the latter resembles the former.

Event Management

The process responsible for monitoring and managing events throughout their lifecycle.

event

Occurrence of an incident raising an alert indicating the disruption of a service.

financial management

The process responsible for providing management with data in order to make the best possible use of its money.

grid computing

A computing model of sharing a complex task across multiple computers.

Help Desk

A point of contact for users to log incidents.

High availability

An approach or design that aims to minimal the effects of configuration item failures for the IT users.

Hybrid cloud

A service that combines the private cloud service with the best services from the public cloud providers.

Hyperic

An application that monitors and manages the performance of virtual, physical, and cloud infrastructures.

IaaS

A service that provides basic computer networking, load balancing, content delivery networks, routing, commodity data storage, and virtualized operating system hosting.

Incident Lifecycle

A design that is used to investigate a specific incident and identify the time to detect, record, and diagnose the incident, and the time to repair, recover, and restore the service.

Incident Management

A process responsible for managing the lifecycle of all incidents. The primary objective of Incident Management is to return the IT service to users as quickly as possible without disrupting the service.

incident

An occurrence of an event against the standard operations which may or may not cause disruption or reduction in the quality of service.

indirect cost

A cost for an activity or service that benefits multiple projects and customers. It is very difficult to measure the value towards a particular project.

information leak/disclosure

A deviation which exposes critical information including system, sensitive or private information, fingerprints and others.

Information Security Management

The process that ensures the confidentiality, integrity, and availability of an organization's assets, information, data, and IT services.

input validation

A process that ensures validation of data conforming to the given application's specifications.

ISMS

(Information Security Management System) A service design approach used to achieve efficient integration of all IT activities and processes, providing end-to-end business-related functionality and quality.

ISO/IEC 20000

An international standard for IT service management, which was developed based upon ITIL processes ensuring that the organization has good IT service management.

IT operations management

A management responsible for the performance of day-to-day activities, operational tasks, functions, and processes.

IT Service Continuity Management

IT Service Continuity Management ensures that the IT service provider can always provide the minimum agreed upon service levels, by reducing the risk to an acceptable level and planning for the recovery of IT services.

ITIL

(IT Infrastructure Library) A community-defined framework and library of IT service management best practices.

ITSM

(IT Service Management) The implementation and management of quality IT services that meet the needs of the business. ITSM is performed by the IT service providers through an appropriate mix of people, process, and information technology.

Knowledge management

A process which ensures that the right information is delivered to the appropriate place or competent person at the right time to enable informed decision making.

KPI

(Key Performance Indicator) A metric that is used to manage a process. While many metrics can and may be measured, only the most important ones are defined as KPIs and are used to objectively measure the progress of a process, service, or activity. This, in turn, gives you the leverage to take an action for improvement.

multi-tenancy

A feature of cloud service which enables multiple users to share the same underlying resources.

network

A group of computers that are connected together to communicate and share resources.

OLA

(Operational Level Agreement) Agreements made between the different departments within an organization.

OSA

(Open Security Architecture) An architecture framework that can be used during the design and integration of security and controls for IT solutions.

PaaS

A service that provides a platform in which to develop software applications with immediate abstractions of the underlying infrastructure.

parallelism as a service

A service provided in the cloud that executes and processes multiple tasks at the same time.

PDCA Model

(Plan-Do-Check-Act Model) A four-stage cycle for process management, attributed to W. Edwards Deming. Also called the Deming Cycle. PLAN: Design or revise processes that support the IT services. DO: Implement the plan and manage the processes. CHECK: Measure the processes and IT services, compare with objectives, and produce reports. ACT: Plan and implement changes to improve the processes.

peer-to-peer model

A network in which resource sharing, processing, and communications control are completely decentralized.

portfolio management

A process responsible for managing a service portfolio for the sake of making sound investment decisions.

Private cloud

A cloud solution that offers hosted services to a limited number of people within an organization.

Problem Management

The process responsible for managing the lifecycle of all problems. The main objective is to prevent incidents and troubleshoot them and reduce the impact of those incidents that cannot be prevented.

problem

A cause of one or more incidents.

process transformation level

The intermediate level at which an organization can introduce new and improved business processes by leveraging the common and scalable assets, and collaborative potential of cloud computing.

Public cloud

A cloud solution in which services are delivered from a third party service provider to the client via the Internet.

release and deployment management

The process responsible for both release management and deployment.

release

A collection of hardware, software, documentation, processes, or other components required to implement one or more approved changes to IT services. The contents of each release are managed, tested, and deployed as a single entity.

Remediation

Recovery to a known state after a failed change or release.

Request Fulfilment

A process that allows the user to log requests, approves, and provides them all requisite information about the log request including general information of services, complaints and comments, and status of the request.

rights

Entitlements, or permissions, granted to a user or role. For example, the right to modify particular data, or to authorize a change.

risk analysis

A process wherein data is gathered to identify the potential threats by assessing the value of the assets and vulnerabilities associated with them.

risk management

A process that involves the identification, selection, and adoption of countermeasures justified by the identified risks.

risk
A possible event that could cause harm or loss, or affect the ability to achieve objectives. A risk is measured by the probability of a threat, the vulnerability of the asset to that threat, and the impact it would have if it occurred.

ROI
Return on Investment is a cost metric used to evaluate the efficiency of an investment.

SaaS
(Software as a Service) A computing model that deploys software over a network, typically the Internet.

SaaS
A service that provides a software solution to the clients. The software may be internal to a business delivered over the Internet.

SACM
The process responsible for both configuration management and asset management.

Scalability
The capability of the cloud service and application to expand or contract the required computing, networking, and storage resources based on need, without human intervention or additional cost.

scale-out architecture
An architecture model that splits the workload over multiple servers so that each server handles only a smaller percentage of load of the overall systems.

scale-up architecture
An architecture model that enables you to scale to larger numbers of processors within a single server.

SCD
(Supplier and Contract Database) An up-to-date record of suppliers, services, and contract details.

SCM
(Service Catalog Management) The practice of maintaining the upkeep of current services, and overseeing the development of potential services.

Service Capacity Management
The activity responsible for understanding the performance and capacity of IT services. The resources used by each IT service and the pattern of usage over time are collected, recorded, and analyzed for use in the capacity plan.

service catalog
A list of services (including the cloud services) and guidelines that are documented, managed, and published by an organization for the benefit of employees or customers. The service catalog includes information about deliverables, prices, contact points, ordering and request processes.

service design
A phase in the IT Lifecycle which provides guidance to design IT services conforming to the best practices and transition the service to live environment ensuring quality in a cost effective way.

service desk
A point of single reference between the service provider and the users.

Service Evaluation
A process which involves the evaluation of all changes made to all services to ensure that there is no potential fallout of the predicted outcome of a change against the actual outcome of a change.

Service Level Management
Service Level Management is responsible for ensuring that all IT service management processes, OLAs and underpinning contracts are appropriate for the agreed service level targets. It also monitors and reports on service levels and holds regular customer reviews.

service management
A set of specialized organizational capabilities for providing value to customers in the form of services.

Service Measurement Framework

An integrated Service Measurement Framework defines what information should be gathered and then goes about collecting the data.

Service Measurement

A process that allows you to monitor and measure performance for ongoing processes of all services.

service operation

A phase in the IT Service Lifecycle that constitutes best practices for achieving the delivery of agreed levels of services to end-users and to customers.

service portfolio

The complete set of services that are managed by a service provider. The service portfolio is used to manage the entire lifecycle of all services, and includes three categories: service pipeline (proposed or in development); service catalog (live or available for deployment); and retired services.

service strategy

One of the core ITIL publications title, Service Strategy establishes an overall strategy for IT services and for IT service management.

service transition

A phase in the IT Lifecycle that gives an account of the delivery of all business services into operational use.

Service Validation and Testing

A process that involves testing and validating all services both within and across various levels in an organization. It begins with the specification of service requirements in a service portfolio and testing and validation of all specifications detailed in them.

sharding

A process of breaking a large database into number of smaller databases.

SLA

(Service Level Agreement) A legal agreement between the IT service provider and the customer on the level of provision of service delivered to the customer.

Supplier Management

The process that ensures that all suppliers' contracts support the needs of the business, meeting their contractual commitments.

TCO

Total Cost of Ownership is an evaluation of direct and indirect cost of a product or system useful in the estimation of the total effective costs of an organization.

Technical Management

Technical Management involves people who provide technical expertise and management of the IT infrastructure.

The Open Systems Interconnection model (OSI model)

The model designed to provide a standard for data communication via a group of sever layers.

UC

(Underpinning Contracts) A legal agreement with a detailed description of all conditions and expectations of a service between a service desk and an external supplier.

utility computing

A computing model that offers computing resources as a metered service based on the utility.

utility level

The basic level at which an organization can benefit from lower costs and higher service levels through the availability of elastic computing resources and pay-per-use models.

virtualization

The process of creating virtual versions of each physical server and each virtual server acts like a real server that can run an operating system and all applications as the physical server.

web API
(Web Application Programming Interface) A
set of programming instructions and standards
for accessing a web-based program.

Index

085195 S3PB rev 1.01
ISBN-13 978-1-4246-1941-2
ISBN-10 1-4246-1941-6

9 781424 619412